T0152312

CRYSTAL INTENTIONS

CRYSTAL INTENTIONS

Practices for Manifesting Wellness

Lune Innate & Araminta Star Matthews

Coral Gables

Copyright © 2019 by Lune Innate & Araminta Star Matthews.
Published by Mango Publishing Group, a division of Mango Media Inc.

Cover Design: Elina Diaz
Cover Photo: Krystal Ng
Interior Photos: Lune Innate
Layout & Design: Elina Diaz

Mango is an active supporter of authors' rights to free speech and artistic
expression in their books. The purpose of copyright is to encourage authors to
produce exceptional works that enrich our culture and our open society.
Uploading or distributing photos, scans or any content from this book without
prior permission is theft of the author's intellectual property. Please honor the
author's work as you would your own. Thank you in advance for respecting our
author's rights.

For permission requests, please contact the publisher at:
Mango Publishing Group
2850 S Douglas Road, 2nd Floor
Coral Gables, FL 33134 USA
info@mango.bz

For special orders, quantity sales, course adoptions and corporate sales, please
email the publisher at sales@mango.bz. For trade and wholesale sales, please
contact Ingram Publisher Services at customer.service@ingramcontent.com or
+1.800.509.4887.

Crystal Intentions: Practices for Manifesting Wellness

Library of Congress Cataloging-in-Publication number: 2019944423
ISBN: (print) 978-1-63353-999-0, (ebook) 978-1-63353-998-3
BISAC category code: OCC004000—BODY, MIND & SPIRIT / Crystals

Printed in the United States of America

Table of Contents

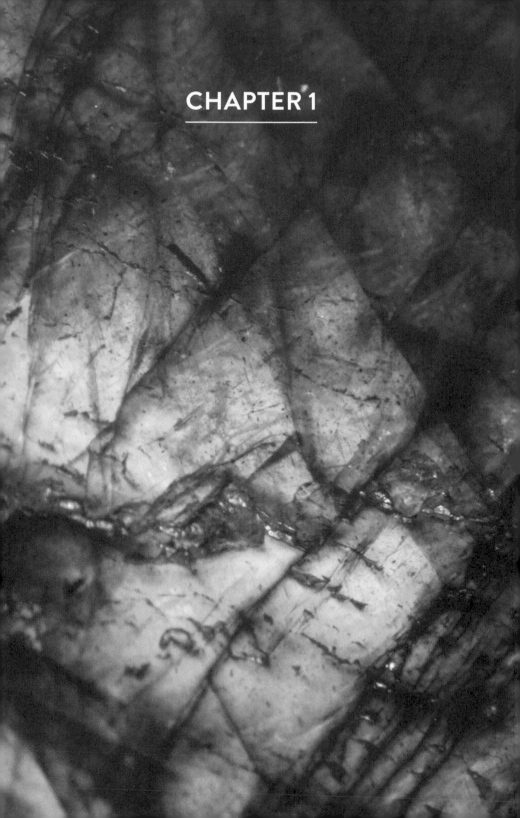

CHAPTER 1

A BRIEF HISTORY OF CRYSTAL VIBRATIONAL HEALING AND POLARITY

Long before crystals and gemstones were part of the New Age Healer's tool kit, they were considered marvels throughout history. They have been mentioned in some way in nearly every religious text from the Hindu Vedas to the Christian Bible, and some archaeologists suggest that the stones themselves were worshipped like gods. A prehistoric dolmen, for example, is a stone or tomb of an honored hero; to early civilizations, dolmens held sacred significance. Stonehenge is thought to have been built of stones not local to the region that were dragged to that location using unknown prehistoric methods for some mysterious purpose. Petroglyphs and cave paintings dating back tens of thousands of years decorate stone surfaces all over the world. People have valued stones for all of recorded history.

Writing is only about ten thousand years old, originating somewhere around ancient Sumer with cuneiform; writings were originally carved into stone surfaces and tablets. That early stone-etched writing detailed our first heroic story, *The Epic of Gilgamesh*, which itself references stone charms. Later, entire works were devoted to stones and their energetic properties. The Greek historian and philosopher Theophrastus wrote a detailed account of stones around 2,500 years ago, which was later expanded by the historian Pliny the Elder in his work *Natural History*. These two works describe the essence and correspondences of stones as tools for metaphysical transformation.

The many ancient civilizations that held gemstones in high esteem— the Egyptians with their Lapis Lazuli, the Russians with their Amber, the Turks with their Turquoise, and the Aztecs and the Chinese with their Jade—all demonstrate that stones are as sacred to certain cultures as they are to the people who are drawn to them. And, perhaps because these elements sparkle and shimmer as if they had been planted in the earth and sea by divinity itself, stones have long been thought to resonate with the same divine energy that makes the planet turn.

The same energy that we might use to transform a thought to action is the very same energy that creates all matter—though a thought lasts only a few moments and a crystal takes millions of years to form. Intentions are thoughts, and actions are manifestations of thoughts in the same way crystals are manifestations of the energy of the Earth. The twelfth century Catholic abbess Hildegard von Bingen used crystals for healing based on her belief that rocks had been created by the "Holy Father" before people and therefore were closer to His healing love. Her notion of *viriditas*, or "greening of the soul," involved using rocks and herbs to energize the spiritual body and heal it from afflictions of the body, mind, and spirit. These notions would be revisited a few hundred years later with the influx of lapidaries, or books about stones, which were devoted to the religious leaders of their times. Now, these same ideas about the energy of stones and crystals are used to improve our overall sense of wellness by those practicing self-care, as well as by energy and crystal healers around the world.

A common question about the use of crystals for healing or manifestation is simply this: How do they work? Of course, we can easily see their beauty and intrigue for ourselves, and we don't need any historical references or ancient artifacts to marvel at them. At the very least, a well-placed crystal can add an element of nature's gorgeousness to our coffee tables. But how might stones serve a purpose beyond just their aesthetic impact? When and why might we turn to crystals to energize or relax ourselves or to invoke our own sense of wellness? How can a gemstone bring peace, love, abundance, or vitality to ourselves or those we might be trying to help? How can we most effectively use them?

To answer these questions, we can look to energetic principles that ancient spiritual leaders expressed. The flow of energy in the body described by various cultures as prana, chi, qi, aether, or even the "breath of life" demonstrates the movement of energy in the complex web of social interaction and human experience. Underlying that web is a network modern-day scientists call quantum physics or the "laws of conservation of matter and energy,"[1] which is connected to how energy moves in and between actions and people. We can also look at present-day medical or healing ideas about wellness and mindfulness; countless studies show that calming the mind can be a very effective treatment for a variety of health conditions. And, of course, we can look at history and philosophy as well as the lore of stones and the conceptual connections we've carved out of our experiences with them. Perhaps it is best to start with a simple principle that we believe may govern both the cellular structure of crystals and the cellular structure of our own bodies: the Principle of Vibration.

From a historical and literary viewpoint, this idea was perhaps first identified in the hermetic philosophy of a book called *The Kybalion*, which first appeared in print in 1908 under the pseudonymous authorship of a mysterious group called the Three Initiates. The book credits the source of its seven principles, including the Principle of Vibration and the Law of Attraction, to the mythical Hermes Trismegistus (thrice-wise), who is thought to have had many incarnations, including Tehuti of Ancient Kemet and Thoth of Egypt. These writings were said to appear on a stone called the

---

1   A great way to approach quantum physics, which is a highly controversial science, is through stories and documentaries. The film (and its later book version) *What the Bleep Do We Know?: Discovering the Endless Possibilities for Altering Everyday Reality*, by William Arntz, Betsy Chasse, and Mark Vicente, released by HCI Media in 2007, knit together the basics of how electrons behave and the impact that behavior might have on our experience of reality. You also might consider Robert Gilmore's 1995 book *Alice in Quantumland: An Allegory of Quantum Physics*, from Copernicus Books, an imprint of Springer-Verlag New York, LLC. Gilmore uses the well-known story of Alice in Wonderland to approach the basics of quantum mechanics.

Emerald Tablet, creating an immediate connection between these principles and gemstones. Hermeticism itself appeared during the alchemical boom between the fourteenth and sixteenth centuries when scientists and philosophers alike took up the mantle of transforming rock into gold. Alchemical texts are steeped in mystical ciphers and symbols that many modern-day philosophers understand as referring not to a chemical process of transmuting one metal into another, but to a spiritual or psychological process of transforming your own energy into a higher state of being. In other words, alchemy is not about discovering the so-called philosopher's stone but concerns the heroic journey it takes to try to raise the frequency of your own energy and the incredible impact such a journey has on your unique vibration as a person.

The concept of vibrational energy within all matter—even crystals and people—resonates both with religious texts and modern science. The Rig Veda, written around 1100 BCE, is one of the ancient texts of India that continues to influence modern-day Hinduism. It may have been the first known text to introduce the concept of spiritual energy and its vibration in the energy centers known as chakras, connecting this energy to physical bodies and thereby uniting mind, body, and spirit. Various scientists and philosophers from Aristotle to Newton to Einstein have suggested the controversial theory that at a molecular level, all things are in motion. With the appropriate magnification tools, we can now see atomic particles dance within all forms of matter. No matter how dense or solid something may seem, when you run your hand over the nubbly, grainy surface of a hunk of rose quartz, remember that its molecular foundations include the same materials as your own body. And, while science may support the idea that all matter, including all solids, liquids, and gasses, among them those that compose biological beings like people and bees, is composed of twirling, shaking, spinning particles, it is really the basic interaction with that energetic world that unites the human experience. When we resonate with something, our spiritual vibrations are in harmony and we are attuned. This attunement is in keeping with these religious and hermetic principles of vibration and attraction.

Simply put, the Principle of Vibration is the belief that everything—including all things, from the cells inside our bodies to the stars that dapple the night sky—is in motion. Everything moves. Everything vibrates. You may already know about the Law of Attraction, which is essentially the idea that you reap what you sow. If you invest your energy into being kind, you will experience kindness because "like attracts like," but this is only the start of manifesting wellness.

In a simplified version of the Law of Attraction, our vibration is most effective when it is intentionally set to attract the experiences we desire. Luckily for us, we are each equipped with the ability to read our own vibration and assess where we stand in relation to our goals. We are emotional beings. These feelings tell us where we stand: When we feel "good," things seem to just go "right," and when we are feeling "bad," things just keep getting worse. As you grow and process your own alchemical transformation of self, you can learn to use your emotions to empower yourself and more easily navigate the world. Even the most attuned of us, though, will have those days where we wake up late, rush through our morning routines, hit snarled traffic, spill our coffee on our shirts, and shake our fists in the air in a general state of stress or frustration.

Do you remember the childhood game "hot and cold," where you closed your eyes and moved around, playing a sort of hide-and-seek with a friend who guided you by yelling "cold" when you moved farther away or "hot" when you were nearer the prize? Emotions are similar in that they tell us how far away we are from what we would wish to manifest through aligning ourselves. In order to move in the direction our emotions may be guiding us toward, we must attune to our own vibration and exercise the principles of the Law of Attraction. Learning to master your vibe is a discipline and practice. The more awareness we bring to the process and the more tools we consciously bring to the experience, such as crystals and gemstones, the easier it is to gain comfort and ease through frequent practice.

One often overlooked aspect of the Law of Attraction is that of perspective. If the emotional compass helps us to know if we are hotter or colder in relation to our goals, then perspective helps us to direct our gaze in the right direction. If we think about the abundance of love, we act from love, and therefore we attract love. If our minds are filled with the "lack of love" because we have a desire for love but no relationship or emotion of love, then we move and act from a place of inadequate resources and we remain in that vibration of "not having." If we flip this law away from the idea of vibration and view it from a different lens, we approach the concept of each individual's "gaze."

Consider that where you look determines what you see. If you are facing a room full of people and you are standing at the same level as all of them, then you only see the tall ones. The short ones are out of view, blocked by the shoulders of the tall ones, and your *perspective* is limited to what you see. Another way to think about this is the gaze of "focus." Let's say you are a babysitter or parent at the park, with your attention hyper-attuned to the children in your care. You watch them jump and play on the playground equipment before moving into a rousing game of tag. Your gaze and your focus are both on the children who are with you, and so you aren't looking at the children on the other side of the park who have just walked off into the dark forest with no adult supervision. Later, when you realize what happened, you would feel mortified. You'd say, "But I was *right there. I should have seen it. I should have done something.*"

This is a great example of how perspective dictates experience. In this scenario, *of course* you should be looking at the children in your care. The point, though, is that the direction of your gaze determined what you saw. It also determined what you did not see, which was *everything else* in the park, including the dark forest. The Law of Attraction also includes the idea that we get what we expect to get, and that we base our expectations on what we see. This is important, because our perspective determines things like the love we experience in our lives. We may miss other opportunities in the world around us, or we may continue to focus our gaze in directions that don't serve us, such as grief, rejection, disappointment, or loneliness. Each of these emotions has a place in our lives, and we should accept our experience of them, but there also comes a point when the perspective they create begins to *attract* more of itself when we might instead point our gaze in a new direction and notice something new.

What about the physical or sensory body? Sight is how we interpret the energy of light and the waves and frequencies of color. Our olfactory sense relies on the vibration of the cilia in our noses and a unique energetic process to create our experience of scent. Taste is linked to the way we smell scents in order to experience the energy of flavor. The sensation of touch is an interplay of energies where we literally *sense* the vibration of another physical object, and hearing allows us to sense sounds through waves as they vibrate within our ears. And, in truth, all of our senses tend to work together to communicate our experience of them—we both feel and hear a drumbeat, taste and smell vinegar, see and hear a basketball bouncing, and so on.

Another way to look at the philosophy of vibration is to consider the connection between cause and effect and to remember that energy is responsible for actions and thoughts. Prayer is energy. Hope is energy. Energy is vibrant. Where we put our energy is most likely where we experience our results. At the microcosmic level, that can be as simple as intending to have cereal for breakfast, acting on the milk, cereal, and bowl, and experiencing the outcome of eating cereal. On the macrocosmic level, that thought or intention to eat cereal was first placed there by the concept of cereal, which came from the marketing of cereal companies, which came as a result of industry, which occurred in response to resource needs and management in an agricultural society, and so on. Every experience we *generate or manifest* is part of a larger web of manifestation of energy—the social network of choices impacting everything right up to the rafters. Every moment is unique in that a tremendous constellation of choices, energies, materials, and circumstances leads us to achieve any given result in the moment. The principles of vibration are how we use our *intentions* and *perspectives* to support our Will in the Universe. Using these principles is a way for us to focus our hopes on an outcome and pull together our experiences to resonate with our greatest good. It is a way to create order out of chaos—just as the crystal is an ordered matrix of molecules that evolves out of high pressure and heat in the Earth's crust.

Minerals, gemstones, and crystals all have their own unique vibrations. Maybe the right tools could allow us to "hear" each stone as it hums when struck or stroked and to hear if the sound of that humming might either feel harmonious or discordant. Sound, after all, is a vibration, and it has been mystically imagined that the stones of the Pyramids of Giza were sung into place with vibrating, resonating voices so powerful they could have a visible effect. Crystals and stones are hewn from the Earth's crust after what may have been be millions of years in formation. Compared to a fruit fly with its twenty-four-hour life cycle, a crystal's vibration is likely more fixed. This is one of the reasons crystals and gemstones are so useful in relaxation and manifestation work. Because they are often very old and are composed of complex molecular matrices, they will hold their vibration whether they are large chunks of mineral or ground into dust, and we can apply our intentions to these stones for years.

Stones are the most effective when they are in our presence, whether in our gaze, held in our hands, or worn on our bodies as jewelry. Just holding a stone in your hands for a few minutes can be enough to match your energy to the vibration of the stone.

Our vibration can change from moment to moment. Our thoughts, actions, and physical states all play a part, but we are also influenced by our environment and by other people. Being in a stressful workplace with a demanding workload or spending time around a friend who seems to only speak to you when she is complaining about her unhappy marriage are examples of outside influences or vibrations that can have an effect on our energy. These are situations we have to navigate, and, because our energy is not fixed, we must be careful and in tune with ourselves. We might absorb the vibration of stress and discord resonating from a burdensome workplace or from an unhappy friend. The good news is that we can raise our vibration through intention setting and gemstone work, and we can even learn to vibrate in such a way that we change the burden of that workplace or raise up the energy of our friend through actions like grounding, centering, mindfulness, manifestation, and relaxation. The trick to this and all energy work we may do with gemstones, herbs, oils, or anything is simply this: conscious intention and action lead to manifestation. With this simple guideline, we can use gemstones to achieve a stronger sense of wellness. Gemstones are a simple, beautiful, and effective method of supporting your vibe.

There are many ways to work with gemstones and minerals, but the most effective is to carry a stone in your pocket or wear one near your skin set in jewelry. As you go about your day, you will likely be experiencing individuals and situations which could perhaps be difficult or out of alignment with your goals and intentions for your highest self and the highest outcome for those around you. Particularly at the start of our personal, alchemical journey to energetic wellness, it is not practical to think you will navigate your day-to-day life unfazed by others. In an ideal situation, we would be able to identify the cause of the stress and transmute it into a life lesson or some type of benefit to our community, but we do not yet live in an ideal set of circumstances. Wellness and relaxation are a path we walk, seeking mastery of the self and perhaps the opportunity to spread that wellness to the community around us. But even the most diligent of us will experience triggers which cause emotional reactions and have the potential to derail positive momentum.

As we develop our affinity for relaxation, mindfulness, and wellness with gemstones, it will be important to remember the principles of vibration and the Law of Attraction. Simply put, we can harness our energy by directing it, just as, when we meditate and our minds become cluttered with the noise of thoughts, we achieve success simply by redirecting the flow. You cannot control every little thing in your world, but you can gently ask yourself to commit and recommit to your intentions. Set a goal, infuse that goal into the stone you are carrying, and return to that goal when you find yourself adrift. Relax. Breathe. Become aware of the stone again, feel its coolness against your skin. Remember what the stone represents to you. Realign, focus your energy, choose your perspective, and begin.

CHAPTER 2

WHAT IS VIBRATIONAL ENERGY? CRYSTALS, ENERGY, VIBRATION, AND HEALING

If you are turning to crystal healing to help relax or experience wellness, you may already have a good footing in the Law of Attraction, and you may have already used crystals to set intentions and help you with the reminding aspect of attraction. Many times, though, our energy work clients come to us missing a step in that process. "I don't understand it. How am I supposed to *feel love* before I have love in my life? How can I create that feeling so that I can attract it? If I already had love, I wouldn't need help attracting it, now, would I?" If you think about it, it's a valid question. You need love to attract love? How does that work? We have found that the missing element in this process is the Principle of Vibration and how that principle can help us to shift our inner dialogue, energize our goals and desires, and become solution-focused so that we may target our truest aspirations with crystal clarity.

Have you ever experienced déjà vu, the notion that you've experienced something before? Or perhaps you've had a premonition when your gut was screaming at you to slam on the brakes even though you couldn't give a clear reason why? Or perhaps you met a person for the first time who just gave you the heebie-jeebies and you couldn't offer a reason at all other than to say, "That person's vibe was slimy"? What if these experiences are simply our evolved body's way of sensing vibration?

Human senses evolved to keep us alive, to survive the stress of a tiger attack all the way to the stress of corporate downsizing. What if your senses achieve this through a complex series of body functions that early humans had no way to observe? Now imagine that you can sense things before you observe them cognitively. Does that sound like magic? Or could it be just a highly evolved sense of intuition?

People have a much less concrete nature than gemstones and crystals. Your vibration, energy, and mood all can potentially change from moment to moment. Your thoughts and actions can be influenced by your environment or by being around other people. Being in a stressful workplace or with people who regularly complain are common examples of outside influences affecting your energy. Because our energy is not fixed, if we are not aware of the way we feel when we interact with that stressful workplace, we will easily succumb to misalignment and the vibration of stress and discord.

At the most basic level, the Law of Attraction suggests that your vibration can be most effective in a frequency which will attract to you the experiences you desire. Luckily for you, we are equipped with the ability to read our own vibration and assess where we stand in relation to our goals. We are emotional creatures. These feelings can act like a barometer to indicate the weather of our internal experiences. When you are feeling joy or cheer, things seem to just go "right." When you are feeling frustrated or sad, it may feel like the day goes from bad to worse. Your emotions can offer a way to measure your metaphysical pulse on the types of experiences you may attract or reject during the day. To shake off the vibration of frustration, you will need some kind of intervention, like a crystal meditation, because now that frustration is what's in your head. It takes a lot to get out of a negative mood. In the field of positive psychology, some studies suggest that negative emotions or "bad vibes" take longer to dissipate than the good vibes, and it can take as many as four positive emotional situations to rebalance a single negative one[2]. Abraham Hicks has stated that the best thing you can do on a day like that is go back to bed.

At any time in your day that you are feeling uncomfortable emotions such as fear, anxiety, jealousy, rage, sadness, guilt, or frustration, you might see it as a signal that you are starting to go off track or moving away from what you desire to attract. It is important to feel our feelings all the way through and even lean into them, such as when grieving the loss of a loved one, and these emotions can also tell us where we are along the path. If you feel sad, it's okay to feel sad; it also might be a signal that you should make a change. For instance, if you find yourself feeling gloomy when you first wake up in the morning and your thoughts go to the drudgery of your workplace, maybe that sadness is trying to tell you it's time to look for a new job. On the other side of the spectrum, when you feel content, joyful, happy, or peaceful, this might be a signal that you are moving toward the goals you have set for yourself either internally or externally. When you feel good, it can be a sign that you are making choices that support your greatest good. If you wake up and feel happy and ready to start the day, perhaps your home or your workplace are the best they can be right now and that joy is a signpost reflecting that.

Of course, this is an oversimplification, because there are so many ways that emotions may behave differently than you expect or ways that circumstances beyond your control can influence your emotions. Fundamentally, though, the emotional center is a compass—an instinctual, internal guiding system. As you move in the direction of your dreams, you should begin to experience harmony. Things should feel easier, and your desires and values should become clearer. Learning to master your vibe is a discipline and a practice. In other words, it doesn't happen overnight; you have to keep at it, bring

---

2 Baumeister, Roy F., Ellen Bratslavsky, Catrin Finkenauer, and Kathleen Vohs. *Bad Is Stronger Than Good.* Review of General Psychology, Vol. 5, 2001. Pp. 323–370. These researchers examined the impact of perceived "bad" emotions on long-term self-satisfaction and found remarkable results about the impact of positive intention and affirmation on wellness.

awareness to it daily and mindfully, and use the tools available to you that will help you regain that frequency of comfort and ease.

Gemstones and minerals each have their own frequency and can be those very tools. You can learn to work with them to stabilize your vibration by aligning your own movement with the frequency or subtle movement of the stone you are using. Hold a stone in your hand which resonates with you personally. If Quartz Crystal does nothing for you, don't use it. Even if this book suggests that Pearl might be a great mineral to use for generating peaceful emotions, you might have an aversion to Pearls and gravitate to another stone instead. That's fine. What matters is how you feel about it, not what some book or expert says. There are no "right" stones. There are only stones that resonate with you or that don't.

HEART CRYSTAL VIBRATION EXERCISE

For example, Rose Quartz is known to have a vibration of love, comfort, romance, beauty, peace, and compassion. To sit for a few minutes with one nearby or, even more effectively, in your hands may help you bring your energetic vibration into the frequency of those qualities. If you hate pink, though, and holding this stone makes you twitch slightly with resentment, then Rose Quartz is certainly not going to help you bring in love and comfort. If you do experience an aversion to a stone, set it aside. It may serve another purpose on another day, but, for now, you need to trust yourself. Try holding different stones until you find one that does make you smile with self-love and compassion when you hold it. Who knows? Maybe for you, the stone of self-love is Jasper or even Petrified Wood. Go with it. This is *your* vibration. You're the only one who can possibly know if it's the right stone for you and your goal.

Since we know solids, liquids, and gasses are composed of moving particles, imagine all the subtle ways you pick up on vibration. As we covered in the History of Crystal Healing, all of your senses are interpreting subtle vibrations, sometimes beneath your conscious awareness. Picture the sound wave or feel the rattling sensation of a drum. Gemstones can be used as a vibrational tool and energetic support. Music and sound therapy, aromatherapy, color therapy, and bodywork such as yoga, massage, and reflexology are also easily accessible tools with which to develop a practice to raise your vibration.

There is a purpose to raising your vibration. When your vibration is humming at a frequency which serves your needs, you are able to move in ways that do not limit you. Decisions you make out of fear are made without clarity of purpose from a thought that something is too difficult. You must be proactive about your vibration. In this disempowered state, you may feel that you are a victim of circumstance and begin to see yourself *as these emotional states.* In no way are we minimizing the impact of mental health concerns, any more than we would wish to minimize physical health concerns. Conditions like depression and anxiety require qualified intervention, in the same way as conditions like cancer or multiple sclerosis do. Having said that, when you start to believe we *are* our conditions— "I'm just a depressed person," or "There is no known cure for MS, so I'm only ever going to be sick,"—you start to internalize this belief, and it can impact your energetic experience as well. Anxiety, for example, can take over and become part of a person's identity, impacting how she sees herself and the world around her.

In addition to medical and therapeutic interventions to support positive health when experiencing anxiety, a person might consider also working on her energetic body and vibrational state. When she internalizes anxiety, she is also sending out a frequency throughout the day. Because anxiety is at the top of her mind, she will see her anxiety everywhere around her—a bit like a projection, which we describe in more detail in the chapter on meridians. Because she is projecting a vibrational energy of anxiety, it will be harder for her to see things which are not resonating at an anxious frequency. Even people who interact with her are likely to sense the vibration of her anxious energy and may unintentionally return that energy to her. It might make them uncomfortable even if they can't pinpoint why in their conscious minds. As we said previously, our senses can subtly experience what our conscious minds may not register, and so other people may be encountering someone's anxiety even if she never says a word aloud. Have you ever been in the room with someone who you could just sense was furious or disengaged, even if that person didn't speak to you? You might say, for example, that you sensed the "vibe"? This experience may occur when you are in the presence of a person who has internalized her mental or emotional state. Many individuals are highly empathetic and pick up on other peoples' vibration or that of an environment, and we can help others *and ourselves* by operating from a place of nonjudgment.

NONATTACHMENT CRYSTAL MEDITATION

Quartz Crystal is an excellent tool to assist with the process of nonattachment. In short, nonattachment refers to a practice of objective observation of our own experiences. When you feel something because someone does something awful to you, it's time to practice nonattachment. For example, let's say you packed a special lunch of leftovers and put it in the fridge at work labeled with your name. Later in the day, you discover that the sandwich is missing and the wrapper is in the trash. Now you are hungry and hurt that your lunch is gone, and you might also feel violated or betrayed by someone who works with you. It would be natural to *feel* sad and angry in this moment. Nonattachment, though, can transmute your feelings of sadness or anger by allowing you to observe them rather than become them. To do this, you imagine you have a third-party observer—your perfect judge, wielding their gavel and adorned in their robes. This observer steps back from you and your experience and remains objective. In this case, the observer would tell you that you have a right to feel sad and angry and that there are lots of different reasons why a person might take your lunch—perhaps a member of your office misread the label and thought she brought the sandwich last week. Perhaps the person who took it was overwhelmed and so distracted that he didn't see the label before he was eating it; or perhaps the person who took it was food insecure and didn't have enough food to pack her own lunch.

The point is that the objective observer steps away and interprets the vibration of the experience in a safe way for us. We can use crystals to accomplish this practice. You might carry a point of Quartz Crystal in your pocket. When you encounter an emotional moment, pull the crystal out and set it on a tabletop nearby. Take a moment with the crystal to set your intention that it will help you process your emotional state. Take five deep breaths: breathe in through the nostrils for a count of four, pause for four seconds, and then out through the mouth for a count of eight. Now, move your perception into the crystal. That is, use your imagination to see yourself from the "eyes" of the crystal; another way to put it is to imagine that the crystal is a benevolent being that is observing you and your surroundings to offer a new perspective. Ask the crystal what it sees, how it feels, and why it feels that way, and ask how can you consciously disidentify from those feelings and the situation without dishonoring the emotions you are feeling. Take a few minutes with this process. Some people may even choose to talk out loud to the crystal and imagine the responses they receive. Others may have a dialogue in their heads, and still others may experience this entirely as impressions or sensations. There's no wrong way to do this. You'll know this crystal exercise has been successful if you feel a sense of relief or calm. Lastly, it bears noting that, most of the time, our Crystal Judge will tell us that the answer to the situation is to practice *compassion*. This process of moving perception into a crystal often triggers an increased ability to feel and express compassion.

This same practice of compassionate nonattachment with a Crystal Judge can be used for ourselves, though many people find it easier to begin with an external event such as the great office sandwich theft. Take a moment to reflect back on the woman who has internalized her anxiety and is seeing, feeling, and experiencing her anxiety in every environment. What if she were to do this exercise at the first inkling of anxiety? Could it help her reframe and perhaps alter her vibration? Not becoming attached to even the feelings or the beliefs we have about ourselves can help us to vibrate in tune with our greatest good. Ever feel like the world is out to get you no matter how hard you try? In these moments, we tend to squeeze harder when what we may really need to do is loosen our grip. Try this crystal exercise the next time you feel disappointed by an experience. Bring in your objective Crystal Judge, move your perspective, and look at the situation through this alternate lens. What changes? Are you able to feel more compassion for yourself?

Compassion is an emotion and supportive concept that we should exercise as much with ourselves as with other people. It seems we all tend to be hardest on ourselves—we expect more from ourselves than we do from others, and we may forget that this process can also help with our own situations. Remember that you are inclined to pick up or sense the vibration of other people. Remember, too, that other people are inclined to sense your vibration. One of the simplest ways to improve your day and bring joy to others is to remember this inclination and practice compassion as you tend to your vibrational energy. All life is interconnected whether we want it to be or not, and our choices have a cause and effect ripple that is immeasurable.

Having a bad day? Snapping at the clerk behind the counter spreads your bad day to him, and then, when he goes home and snaps at his daughter, it spreads it to her. Because we all share experiences, it is critical that we raise our collective vibration by staying in alignment with our personal goals and values as much as possible so that we can resonate in tune with our vibrational energy.

As you go through your day and encounter the stress or joy of other people and situations, these experiences may not be in alignment with your personal desires. Or perhaps more accurately, the way you feel about or respond to these experiences may not be attuned. As a novice vibrational energy worker, it is not practical to think that you will navigate your day to day unfazed by any stressors, obstacles, or others' energy. In an ideal situation or after many months or years of vibrational practice, you can identify the cause of the stress and transmute it into a lesson or some type of benefit. Often, for example, the Crystal Judge exercise may help you identify a reason for gratitude for your situation as well as compassion. Gratitude helps us to recognize what we are working to transmute from negative to positive through positive psychology and crystal healing. At the same time, even at your most diligent, you are still subject to emotional triggers which have the potential to derail the positive momentum.

Thus far, we've been exploring the notion of transmuting or objectively observing so-called "negative" experiences and how crystal meditation can assist, but it is worth mentioning now that the types of language used for discussing energy, vibration, spiritual concepts, and wellness are not exactly unified. The terms "negative" and "positive" reflect the science of magnets, but the terms themselves have a connotation of "bad" and "good," even though this is not how they are intended here. A negative pole is the side of the magnet that pushes outward while the "positive" pole draws inward. Another way to view the negative and positive poles without judgment is to conceptually align them with the yin and yang concepts of void and substance. Both states are necessary for creation and manifestation. For example, negative is associated with yin energy, receptivity, and intuition. This is the state of possibility. Positive is linked to yang energy, action, and expression, or the state of form. These two forces are at play within us every moment of the day, and they are only "bad" or "good" by virtue of how we choose to interpret and respond to them. Together, they are the inner thought or feeling as well as the outward action or reaction; they are the ability to receive as well as to give. These forces which seem so opposite are in fact simply the movement of energy and vibration along the spectrum of one pole to another, just as the tides ebb and flow or the Moon seems to disappear and be reborn with each rotation of the Earth. It is a dance necessary for movement.

Now apply the same principle to the polarity of our energetic experiences, such as emotions, physical states, or thoughts. Many spiritual and lifestyle teachers agree about the importance of a nonattached view of both positive and negative poles. These poles may seem dualistic at first glance, but they are poles at either end of a spectrum with an infinite number of states in between. With this acknowledgment in mind, you may find it easier to shift from discomfort to comfort or from dissonance to attunement with practices like the Crystal Judge. Practicing these concepts can fortify your trust in your agency, and it can help you transform an uncomfortable situation into one that serves you. Your ability to master your vibrational interpretation of these experiences is the key to ensuring that your experiences, whether they are void or substantive, can help move you toward your highest good.

You might imagine that every situation you experience *should* be pleasant or just or righteous. Why not? So-called unpleasant experiences cause pain or discomfort. Nonattachment and the Crystal Judge can help you separate from the desire or "need" to control. Engaging in objective observation can help you move your perspective from what is narrowly in front of your face at the moment to the larger picture of what is happening around you or what may occur in the future. Shift your perspective to take in the bigger picture rather than only witnessing the "bad" or "good" of an experience. Then you can create the change you need to propel yourself along your path.

You may experience loss, pain, or even anger when a relationship ends. Love can even turn to hatred, but it is important to remember that these are two poles of the same spectrum and the energy may make a pendulum swing back to love at times. The opposite of love is indifference; the energy you choose to spend on feelings is a value you transfer onto someone else. Hatred is just the other side of the love energy spectrum—after all, why expend energy hating someone unless you want to spend that energy? When focused on the end of a relationship, you might get stuck on the details of who was right or at fault, who put in more work, or what your partner should have done.

By taking a step back and witnessing with gratitude and compassion, you can take a new vantage point and realign with your intuition and logic, or what Dialectical Behavior Therapy refers to as your "Wise Mind." In this place, both logic and emotion work together to help you arrive at your best outcome. It is the perfect space from which to vibrate as it is one of clarity and understanding. Zoom out of the experience to see how the experience can serve your highest good and realign your vibrational frequency. Relationships often end when neither partner is able to support the other's goals any longer, or when two people stop growing together in the same direction. The ending of a relationship creates space for support, love, or taking time that you might need in order to feel fulfillment of your truest goals. And sometimes, in this place of reflection and openness, you may realize at your core that you always sort of knew this relationship needed to end in order for both of you to grow and experience your truth. Relationships are not limited to our chosen romantic partners but can include family, coworkers, and friends.

It can help to retune our energy with a crystal ritual to release the energy, forgive yourself and your partner, practice compassion, and open yourself up to new experiences. It can also be helpful to process grief for the relationship's ending, whether that relationship was ended by someone's behavior or by something we cannot control, such as death. Choose any crystal that resonates with you. It should feel peaceful and calm when you hold it in your hands. It might even be warm to the touch or cause you to smile when you touch it. On a slip of paper, write yourself a note to release and reopen. You might say something like, "I am sad that this relationship has ended. I am grateful that this relationship allowed me to learn something, and I will carry that lesson with me. I forgive myself. I feel compassion for you and for me. I release you and all the thoughts and feelings I have about this relationship, and I now open myself to new and joyful experiences." Fold the paper and place it beneath the stone you selected. If you are so inclined, light a candle nearby and watch the light flicker over the stone. Soften your gaze as you observe how the flame dances over the stone's surface. Focus your vision on the stone and focus your sensation on your breath. Stay here as long as you need to feel complete. When you are through, snuff out the candle and tear up the paper, or burn it if you are so inclined and can do so safely. This releases the energy of the note. Now, carry the stone with you as long as you need to remind yourself of your release.

CHAPTER 3

GROUNDING AND CENTERING TO SELF-HEAL, REDUCE BURNOUT, AND RELAX

Before we begin to work with any self-healing method, it is a good idea to ground in the moment, center yourself, and set intentions. "Grounding and centering" is language borrowed primarily from the modern pagan movement, but the principles are recognizably the same as those in most healing, therapeutic, or mindfulness strategies regardless of background or context. The matter of setting intentions allows us to tune into ourselves carefully and ensure that the energy we put into our relaxation work is focused in the direction that serves our greatest good.

Ever feel like you are just working really hard and accomplishing nothing? It's almost as if this is the nature of stress and frustration. We expend all our energy, but it's like revving the engine to try and get a car out of a muddy trench. We just keep spinning our wheels, wearing out the motor and using up all our fuel, only to end up stuck in the same place and covered in mud. Stressful situations—even those stressful situations we invite into our lives, such as the stress of a new project or job—deplete our energy supply both in the activities related to the stress and in our efforts to relax and calm things after the fact. Relaxation, of course, is necessary both in happy situations and unhappy ones, because we cannot stay at high velocity permanently. Energy, though limitless in nature, is finite within the human subtle body field, as it must be restored to maintain harmony and balance. You reach your best state of wellness when you become aware of both the present state of your stress levels or overall energy and the knowledge that you have the power within yourself to restore peace within.

The social, physical, and emotional demands of life have increased over the past several decades. Over a century ago, during the dawn of the industrial revolution that made our supply of food, water, and resources more efficient and pulled people out of the farm fields and into the factory, early students of sociology began to examine the nature of labor and commerce, concluding that the critical thing people had to exchange for food and water was their *time*. Not everyone could be wealthy or born into royalty, and so survival of the poor and working classes depended on our ability to trade one commodity for another. Since the poor tended not to have land or objects to trade for resources, they came to trade their time for the financial resources necessary to survive. It was during the early days of this social experiment, when the labor forces were unable to till the fields and instead found opportunity in the factories, that we began to recognize the impact and value of labor in terms of its toll on our bodies. Labor takes time and energy, and that energy is depleted from our bodies and must be restored consistently.

Labor and energy go into many more activities than simply those that earn us the financial resources we need to eat, drink, sleep, and remain safe. Labor and energy go into all our activities, whether they be studying for that big biology exam tomorrow, caring for the needs of a houseful of toddlers, packing up our household possessions to move across the country, or even going on vacation.

Mental pursuits, such as programming software applications or designing websites, also expend our labor and energy. Unlike the industrial revolution, during which we moved from farm fields to the Ford assembly line, this technological revolution has had a tremendous impact on our bodies and minds. Even though we are not toiling in coal mines beneath the ground or riveting bolts into the beams of a skyscraper a mile above it, we are still expending energy on the hidden costs of our new technologies—and of our addiction to them. While modern technology has given us the potential to research any topic, work at our professions remotely, or source inspiration for our next meal, it has a downside. It is difficult to unplug; we reply to emails at two in the morning when we should be sleeping, or we spend hours mindlessly scrolling through social media with little awareness of how the images or messages we're absorbing might be affecting our psyche, let alone our vision or our sleeping patterns.

On one side of the burnout spectrum, we have stress which occurs when we expend our energy in hyperactive ways. Stress is a form of anxiety that stems from the "fight" part of our fight-or-flight instincts left over from our tiger-fighting days. Stress rises when we experience a rushed need to expend energy in a difficult situation, such as managing conflicting priorities or saving lives during a natural disaster. It also arises when we experience the need to expend energy for positive situations, such as finishing that painting or playing basketball with your friends.

Prolonged stress results in burnout. It is the exhaustion of your energetic body where you disengage both mentally and physically. Burnout resembles depression; with both, you feel less interested in things and people. When you are burned out, your body—both at the subtle and physical levels—is crying out for you to slow down and let things cool off for a while so you may return to your optimal energetic state.

Many psychological professionals see burnout as a symptom of poor stress management. Spending excessive screen time with video games, social media, and television keeps you engaged mentally even if you are sedentary, and you deplete your energy trying to unwind by winding right back up again. What's more, a recent study by a major health insurance provider found that the current generation is more lonely than any other generation in history.[3] Part of the blame for that loneliness, which is a state of burnout, belongs to our devotion to technology as an attempt to replace our very real needs for direct human contact and social engagement. That lack of in-person socialization has a profoundly negative impact on your well-being.

We may begin to feel lost and isolated without meaningful relationships. It can feel as if we are missing something of great importance in our lives. This also can lead to being too much "in our own heads," and even simple social interactions become overwhelming. This can make it even more difficult to form connections, and we may take things too seriously or personally. Healthy relationships manifest more easily when navigated from a calm and balanced state.

Crystal relaxation strategies can help center that energy by winding down your stress or restoring your energy after the depletion of burnout has set in. Developing awareness about our current energy state and the onset of stress and burnout is the best defense. Set an intention and choose an action—even non-action—to restore comfort and peace, lead to your own greater clarity, and reverse the "downward spiral." Energetically speaking, even the smallest of shifts in the right direction can truly turn the tide.

Stress and burnout certainly affect us in our physical bodies as we experience tension or exhaustion. Sometimes we even experience these physical symptoms of burnout in the form of pain, which is like a warning flare sent by our bodies to alert us that something is wrong: if we keep going at a certain pace or remain in our current condition, we might do actual damage to our bodies. But what are the cues that we receive from the energetic realms within our *subtle* bodies?

---

3   Douglas Nemecek, Chief Medical Officer for Behavioral Health, Cigna. *Cigna US Loneliness Index: Survey of 20,000 Americans Examining Behaviors Driving Loneliness in the United States*, 2018.

There is an ancient saying that can help explain the impact that physical energies can have on our subtle energies: *As above, so below, and as within, so without.* The origins of this concept have been credited to multiple sources, including the Emerald Tablets associated with Egyptian and Greek mythology. Mystery surrounds these alchemical messages inscribed on green stones, but the earliest known reference to these arcane texts occurred around the eighth century; interest in them was later reinvigorated by medieval alchemists[4] and then again by the unique blend of transcendent psychology uncovered by Carl Jung. References to the concept expressed by "As above, so below" occur in many religious writings, including the Christian Bible, the Tao Te Ching, the Vedas, and many other sacred texts throughout history.

This ancient saying expresses the concept of correspondence between the inner and outer worlds of being. This idea is reflected (or perhaps refracted) by the crystal. The outside of a crystal is beautifully structured, and the inside of a crystal is a perfect geometric pattern. Everything without and within (above and below) is in alignment. Energy is similarly experienced: When you are feeling disconnected from your experience of the divine, your outer energy in your physical body is low, and you may present to others with a duller tone or less of that twinkling inner fire that burns within you. You may become sick or exhausted as your inner world is reflected through your body to the outside world. The same is true in reverse: when you are sick or agitated physically, you may experience emotional symptoms that may present a withdrawn or disorganized appearance to others, as though your *Self* is disconnected.

This sacred unison of *Self* is reflected by crystals, which come from the ground and thus are excellent tools for *grounding.* They were once thought to be ice, expressing the universal connection between

---

4   Everard, J. (translator from original Arabic document by J.F. in 1650). *The Divine Pymander of Hermes Trismegistus.* New York: Societas Rosicruciana in America, 1952. Reprinted.

earth and water energies. The word itself, "crystal," comes from the
Greek word for frozen water. Your body is a physical expression of
your energetic body, just as crystals are a physical expression of the
organizational energy of the universe. When you are stressed and
your layers of existence are out of alignment, you look to attune your
outside with your inside to realign; "As above, so below." Crystals
can be particularly useful to this because their internal structure is
geometric perfection.

Crystals are actually defined by their internal structure, or the
organization of their atoms and molecules. While it is true that
crystals can be manufactured or mimicked by commercial factories,
we encourage you to work with true, raw crystals which are ethically
harvested from the Earth in sustainable ways so that you can tap the
energy of their geometric perfection. True crystals contain within
them perfectly symmetrical, geometric, interlacing rows of atoms. It
is this internal organization that allows crystals to be such collectors
of energy to power lasers and solar panel cells.[5] That same principle
of inner organization and outer beauty can also be harnessed for
attunement and alignment when you are experiencing burnout or just
need the opportunity to relax. Inner order makes for outer order.

It is possible to achieve energetic balance when both sides of the
burnout teeter-totter are level. In your optimal state, time seems to
fall away, and you achieve what psychologist Mihaly Csikszentmihalyi
refers to as *flow*. Creativity represents the force of love in the universe.
According to Dr. Csikszentmihalyi, flow occurs when there is order
in consciousness and that order breeds creative and loving energy.
Its opposite state, entropy, occurs when we are in a state of disorder.
Flow occurs when your entire consciousness is focused on achieving
your inner goals. Flow exists when you battle "against the entropy that
brings disorder to consciousness. It is really a battle *for* the self; it is a

_____

5   A detailed account of crystal structure for laypeople (or nonscientists) can be found in Richard J.D. Tilley's *Crystals and Crystal Structures*. West Sussex, England: Wiley, 2006.

struggle for establishing control over attention" (Csikszentmihalyi 41).[6] Like the hermetic teachers before him, Csikszentmihalyi identifies the goal of self to be a state of organized alignment between body and energy. Perhaps Csikszentmihalyi, whose own brother achieved flow while studying crystals,[7] might honor crystals for their optimal flow of organized energy within and beauty without.

Like flow, mindfulness is the *awareness* of that state of creative focus. People in a state of flow are so focused on the task of creation that they forget all about the world around them—in some cases, they even forget about their own bodies as attention to pain or hunger slip away. The flowing person transcends the needs of the body, but there is a problem with being in a state of flow for too long. Pain and hunger exist to keep the physical body operating. For flow to be optimal, it must be both hyperfocused on creation (the fight for *self*) and *mindful of it*. But how do you do that? How do maintain an awareness of body, mind, and energy while allowing yourself to engage fully with your state of flow?

Mindfulness is one of the tools we use to weave the fabric of our many selves together into one. While it is a marvel that creative energy can allow your awareness of your body to fall away while you flow with creative energy, returning to your physical body after spending so much time in your energetic body may be a bumpy reentry. Being mindful refers to an intention to be aware of what's happening both within and without. Truly gifted mindfulness practitioners do not judge what that awareness highlights; that is, they attune to what they think or feel in a given moment, but they don't necessarily attach to those thoughts or feelings. Judgment actually takes you out of the moment and causes an interruption to

---

6 Csikszentmihalyi, Mihaly. *Flow: The Psychology of Optimal Experience.* New York: Harper Perennial, 2008 (reprinted edition).

7 Niemiec, Ryan M. "When Mindfulness Trumps Flow: Which Do You Choose when these Two Positive Processes Collide?" in *Psychology Today*, June 11, 2013. Retrieved Oct. 2, 2018, from https://www.psychologytoday.com/us/blog/what-matters-most/201306/when-mindfulness-trumps-flow.

the direction of your energy. The key is to honor and not deny the experiences you have—warts and all.

If you are to manifest your greatest good, you can't be in denial. Denial sends energy to the very thing you are choosing to deny, because denial *is an action*. If you are actively trying to reject something—perhaps because you don't like how it feels—then you are aware of that rejection and your thoughts and reality will be out of alignment. An example of this we see often is the client who says she wishes to attract something into her life—we'll say more joy and happiness—but continues to engage in the activities that cause her to feel unhappy. She knows she wants more happiness and works with her crystal healer to manifest it, but, subconsciously, she denies the need to make changes in herself to be *aware of that happiness.* Manifesting wellness takes intention and a willingness to change.

Grounding with a crystal connects you to the present. It might literally mean connecting with the ground beneath you, which is always supporting you by holding you up, feeding your body, and quenching your thirst. Most gemstones and minerals are sourced from the ground; even organics like Pearls, Jet, and Amber are connected to Earth in some capacity. In fact, 12 percent of the Earth's crust is made up of silicon dioxide or Quartz Crystal, making it the most plentiful gemstone on the market[8]. Perhaps this is why grounding with a crystal in each hand as you stand with your feet connected to the Earth amplifies your energetic connection, as though the crystals you hold are charged and generating a connection to the crystals beneath our feet in the ground below.

---

8   Morgan, Diane. Gemlore: Ancient Secrets and Modern Myths from the Stone Age to the Rock Age. Westport, CT: Greenwood, 2008. P. 150.

GROUND AND CENTER

If you are able to stand, consider grounding on your feet so that you can cycle the energy of the Earth up through your spine and back down again into the ground as if you are pushing your feet down like tree roots into soil. If you are unable to stand, you can accomplish a similar grounding experience by lying flat on your back and noticing where your body makes contact with the ground beneath you. If you have access to nature, it is best to do this directly on the unpaved, unaltered ground in its natural state so you can connect closely with the energy of the planet. You can also achieve that connection while on a floor or a bed with a little extra work by consciously remembering that the Earth is below you.

The imagination is a powerful grounding tool. Try this visualization to emotionally cleanse yourself. Imagine that you are standing under a glittery, rushing waterfall. The water pours over an outcropping of rocks into a clear, blue pool warmed by the sunlight. The spray of the waterfall creates a mist dappled with rainbows everywhere you look. Imagine yourself standing beneath this flow of crystal-clear water as it washes away your stress and frustrations. Feel your feet sink slightly into the water of the pool as your toes flex to grip the stony earth beneath them.

The key to grounding is to pause and pay attention to where you are connected to the ground. Choose two or more crystals and place one in each of your hands. If you are flat on your back, you might also place a crystal on your Third Eye between your eyebrows, over your heart, and near your pelvis to cycle energy along your chakras as well. Some people even place a crystal beneath their feet while standing or lying down.

If you have a few gemstones you wish to bring into your practice but are not sure where to place them, try this quick connecting exercise.

Take each stone individually and hold it so that it hovers a few inches above the skin, about where you imagine your aura might be. Starting at the top of the head, slowly move the stone down along the center of the body and sense where it "wants" to go. Pay attention to where it may feel pulled to your body, as if by a light magnet. You might be surprised. The Red Jasper that many associate with the deep red Root Chakra may feel drawn to the space above your heart, or a Blue Apatite traditionally associated with the Throat Chakra might tug magnetically toward your Solar Plexus instead. There are no rules when working with gemstones. Just *listen* to them.

Focus on the sensation of your body rather than the emotions or thoughts you might be having. Sensation is your physical experience. It is the points, rough-hewn edges, or polished surfaces of the crystals you feel in each of your hands. It is the coolness of the stone on your forehead (or warmth, in the case of Amber). It is the sharp, forceful pressure in your feet as you notice each bone and muscle in your soles flexing and pressing into the ground beneath you. In turn, you should experience the Earth rising to hold you up.

There is an old Buddhist proverb that goes something like, "The foot becomes the foot when it feels the ground beneath it." Essentially, this refers to the awareness that we experience when we recognize sensation. Don't judge or interpret as you might with emotions and thoughts. In fact, if thoughts float into your head, acknowledge them and brush them to the side as you refocus your energy into experiencing the sensations of your body. Feel your feet, and know that they are feet by the ground that you feel beneath them. Know that you are the ground by your feet above them. Feel the rise and fall of your breath in your chest. Ground by *tuning in to your material self.* Experience your own physical surface as it relates to the world around you—your skin, your breath, your muscles, your blood. Ground by pushing your energy into the Earth and the crystals you feel with your body. Ground by pulling that same energy up from the Earth as if you are drawing water from the roots of a tree and pulling it in.

Grounding is connecting with the surface of yourself, and centering is connecting with the core of yourself. When you ground, you feel the crystals in your hands. For balance, you can hold a Clear Quartz point in your receptive hand to amplify the energy you draw in and a piece of Smoky Quartz or Black Kyanite in your dominant hand to transmute the energy you are expelling, but use whatever stones *speak to you personally*. When you center, take that energy from the crystals and *breathe* it into the center of the body. Draw that energy inward by imagining it flowing into you through your breath, and then guide that breath to the parts of your body where you wish it to go.

Draw energy into your heart by shifting your focus from physical sensation to emotion, or from your body to your heart. Experience the calmness of your body by replicating the physical sensation of calm with the same emotional state. You can guide your emotions in this way. Choose crystals that resonate with your energy centers to help you draw that energy within you. Chakras will be explored more thoroughly later in this book, but, for now, imagine that your spine is a rainbow starting with deep red at your pelvic floor and ending with vibrant purple radiating from your head. Choosing stones that make you think of love or that align with your Heart Chakra can help, and you might place them directly on your body, either just resting there or set in jewelry, like a necklace. Good stones for love and trust are Rose Quartz, Pink Agate, or Chrysoprase (perhaps shaped like hearts or engraved with hearts, as a general concept), or, alternatively, stones that are green to represent *Anahata*, the heart energy center. These might include Jade, Epidote, Green Opal, Aventurine, Green Calcite, or Emerald—just beware, some stones (like Malachite) can be toxic to the touch or when ingested accidentally, and other stones (like Rose

Quartz or Opal) can lose their luster if exposed to excessive sunlight.
Opal in particular can have a dried-out appearance if exposed to the
elements too long due to the fact that as much as 10 percent of an
Opal's chemical composition is actually water that can leach out of
the stone over time.[9]

After selecting stones to employ in centering, infuse both the stone
and your breath by tuning into yourself to prepare for manifestation.
Breath, chi, or prana is an important aspect of crystal healing, as it
is the energy that flows in and out of our bodies. Breath can also be
whispered into a stone. Hold a stone close to your lips and whisper
your intention into it, then breathe it in deeply as if you are sniffing a
sea rose in full bloom.

PRANAYAMA EXERCISE

Try this quick breathing technique to align your breath. You're going
to breathe in a 4:4:8 count. Begin by drawing in a breath for four
seconds. Hold that breath in your lungs for four seconds, and then
breathe out for eight seconds. Count out the numbers in your mind
as you breathe: in for four, hold for four, out for eight. Keep breathing
this way for a few minutes or until you feel relaxed and attuned to
your body. By breathing out for a longer stretch of time than you
breathe in, you will sink your body into relaxation by pushing out the
toxins. It almost feels like you are lowering as your shoulders drop
and your jaw releases tension. You can also alternate breathing in and
out through each nostril to deepen your focus while you count. Draw
in through the right for four, hold, breathe out through the right for
eight, and then repeat with the left.

9   Opal has a long history in gemlore, and there are references to Opal in lapidaries (books about stones and crystals)
     dating back thousands of years. Opal is one of the few stones that actually contains water within itself (which is part
     of its sparkle), and it is actually a hydrated silica gel. Even though it contains so much water, it has a Mohs Hardness
     scale of about 6, which makes it safe to cleanse in water or olive oil. Diane Morgan's acclaimed work, Gemlore, is a rich
     resource about many gems, including the magnificent Opal. Morgan, Diane. Gemlore: Ancient Secrets and Modern
     Myths from the Stone Age to the Rock Age. Westport, CT: Greenwood, 2008.

After whispering an intention or wish into your stone, hold it in your hands and picture a state of pure relaxation. All the muscles in your body have turned to jelly, and your head lolls from side to side on a downy pillow. In this mental picture, as you center yourself, remember that details in the central mind are powerful and can assist with manifestation. Mind your thoughts and allow only those which support your highest good to be of focus. If you notice you are drifting toward a negative image, interrupt it. Clap your hands, or tap your crystal on the ground and say firmly, "Stop!" Forgive yourself for the interruption and return your focus to centering.

Dig deep and imagine your wildest relaxation dream in vivid detail. Do you feel relaxed at the top of a mountain with your metal-cleated shoes clipped into a rock as the icy wind whips your hair around your face? Do you feel relaxed submerged in a pool of Dead Sea mud, heated by hot springs and surrounded by a gentle snowfall while you tip your head back and cover your eyes with cucumber slices? Draw the mental image of that relaxation into your mind, but don't stop there. Imagine you can feel it emotionally and sense it physically, too, and tell yourself you can return to this feeling and sensation anytime you like by revisiting your stone.

Emotional and physical imagination are key factors in centering work as well as manifestation, and the more detailed your imagining of the experience, the easier it will be to manifest later. If you have trouble imagining sensations, try taking an improv or yoga class to attune more acutely to your sensory reactions. For emotional awareness, consider counseling or a poetry class. The more vividly you can conjure up an emotional and sensational experience, the more likely you can manifest it into reality. The number one trick to manifestation is to connect your future goals to something tangible: connect the joy you *hope* to feel with the sensations of joy you once felt in the past. Draw up those joyful emotions and inject them into the goal you are targeting. Picture yourself feeling that joy in the new situation. Make it tangible, and use the crystal as a *reminder* of that goal.

If you are having difficulty focusing on what you want to manifest, try asking yourself. Literally ask yourself out loud, "What do I want?" Or you may choose to write it in a journal, like crafting a letter to yourself, and then await the response. If you feel blocked, try focusing instead on what you want to feel emotionally or as a state of being. Love? Connection? Success? Health? Hope?

One way to prepare your mind is to flip the script upside down. Instead of asking yourself what you want, try to remember what you want as if you are remembering an event that hasn't happened yet. It may seem weird to use the word "memory" here when you're trying to remember something from your future, but we all know time isn't linear, right? We can remember future states, even if they are fictions. In fact, sometimes fictions become the future, like when a fiction writer like Ray Bradbury imagined retinal scanners and flat-screen televisions for his book *Fahrenheit 451* during a time when locks were mechanical and televisions used cathode rays. This *fiction* became a reality when scientists engineered these devices more than fifty years later. Don't be afraid to dream or remember a new future—this is the heart of manifestation. Dream it. Become it.

Use the stone to amplify your experience and do some of the work for you. You might think of stones as programs you script and run on your computer as you prepare them with your intentions. Stones operate like scripts, working beneath the surface to make things run smoothly. A script can be as simple as just the word "relax" said once or repeatedly over the stone. You might feel guided to hold the stone very close to your mouth and speak into it as if you are telling it your deepest, darkest secrets. Some crystal workers take a more alchemical approach and write the intention on a slip of paper that is then wrapped around the stone with ribbons. Infuse the crystal with your intentions to pair its own inner strength with yours as you ground, center, and relax.

CHAPTER 4

VIBRATIONS AND INTENTIONS TO MANIFEST WELLNESS

You can work with a myriad of available gemstones and minerals. No list of gemstones (including the one later in this book) is ever truly complete, because you yourself have significant agency over how you choose to use them. Though we may recommend indigo stones like Lapis Lazuli or Iolite to enhance your intuition, you might find you are more drawn to red or yellow stones like Citrine or Ruby for this work instead. In fact, you may find that color has no significance at all, or that one stone in particular, such as Quartz Crystal, resonates so richly with you that it is the only one in your collection. When it comes to crystal intentions, what matters most is your attunement to your own sense of being. *Listen to your stones. Pay attention to how they speak to you. Develop your own unique rapport with your stones.*

Even with a list of stones and their correspondences for manifestation, new varieties of stone are still being catalogued, such as the ocean-dappled Larimar, which was rediscovered just a few decades ago in the Dominican Republic. And labels for stones change over time, too, so the Quartz Crystal of one generation is the Ice Crystal of another. These new discoveries and labels make it impossible to establish any kind of definitive guide to stones. In fact, we would emphasize the word *guide* here and remind you that guides do not dictate so much as suggest. It may seem helpful to have an idea of what others think of a stone's so-called purpose, but you will find stones resonate with you uniquely. You have your own energetic vibration and a unique body chemistry. In this book, we may offer our experiences with the frequency of each stone as we know it, but it is always important to remember that stones will resonate uniquely with you and what works for one of us may not work for you.

One person may find Amethyst calming or supportive as it helps him to fall asleep when placed under his pillow at night. Another person may feel "buzzy," restless, and destabilized when she holds a piece of Amethyst before bed. Until you hold a stone in your hand, you cannot clearly sense how it makes you feel or if it is the right choice for you at the moment. Ground, center, and attune to your stone to *hear* or *sense* if it is the right one for you right now.

You can carry a grounding stone like Jasper in your pocket or as jewelry, or you can incorporate it into a meditation to support your vibrational energy and stabilization. In this case, the Jasper becomes the tool you will use to create the foundation on which you build your sense of comfort and support. If you are looking to manifest a desire such as the completion of a creative project, you might be inspired to pair Jasper with something you feel resonates with your desire or goal, such as the creative stone Yellow Fluorite. If you are trying to build love or romance on the grounding foundation of Jasper, then you might choose Rose Quartz or Rhodochrosite to attract and support that love. And if you are developing your spiritual senses and intuition, you might select an Anhydrite or Amethyst to build a spire off the ground of the Jasper straight into the metaphorical clouds.

INTUITIVE CRYSTAL DRAWING EXERCISE

The following exercise is a beautiful way to exercise your ability to sense energy and attune to your intuition. This is the Intuitive Crystal Drawing Exercise. Begin by laying out your collection of gemstones and minerals before you, either on a large tabletop or on the floor, whichever is more comfortable to you. Sit for a moment and set an intention for yourself that you will choose the stone which will best support your highest good for the day. If you've never set an intention before, there are a number of ways you can do this. One way is to simply take a moment to make a statement in positive language that articulates your goal or desire. Another way to do it is to follow the SMART acronym, which first appeared in the early 1980s in a management magazine. A SMART goal is a goal which is Specific, Measurable, Achievable, Realistic, and Timely. Creating an intention for your stone involves creating a statement which is all of these things. For example, I might intend to attract love, and so my intention might be a statement I either write or say to myself like so: "I infuse this stone with my desire to attract love, which I will know by feeling light and connected to another person or people before the end of today."

This method of setting an intention, however, may not resonate with everyone. You can also simply remember a time you felt the way you are hoping to feel, such as a time in the past when you felt joyful and loved. You can also imagine what it might feel like to experience that emotion. Get as detailed as you can, pulling in the physical sensations and emotional vibrations you imagine go along with that experience—maybe you imagine you'd taste cookies and smell roses, for instance, or your skin might tingle; whatever it is, really feel it. If these methods still do not resonate with you, you can also simply clear your mind and ask the stone to help you release that which doesn't serve you and attract that which does.

Setting an intention is the first step to working with crystals to manifest and align with our energetic selves. If you plan to carry the stone with you or meditate with it, this might be the intention you speak to the gemstones you laid out before you. Your body has an innate intelligence and will communicate what is desired in a variety of possible ways. With your left arm, slowly wave or drag your hand over the tops of each stone, not touching them. Hover a couple of inches over the tops of them and sense where your hand desires to go, as if it is moving on its own and not being guided by your brain. It will perhaps feel quite subtle, like a dull magnet, or you may sense strong tingles in your palm or warmth moving up your arm. There are no rules for how your senses communicate, and the more you work with these subtle communications, the more easily you will pick them up. Once you have selected your stone, sit with it for a few minutes, and then set your intention to connect with it. Treat this connection as though you are entering into a new relationship—a friendship, for example—and draw up the feelings of support and love as you hold it. You are now ready to carry this stone or place it in a spot where you will see it regularly, such as on your desk.

While it is not a bad idea to simply have gemstones and minerals in your home or carried with you, choosing these stones based only on what you've read or how you've been advised without pairing that information with your own personal intention can actually work against your goals. Setting your intention allows you to dedicate your stone to assist you in some way.

Clear Quartz is an ideal stone to use for virtually any task because it is known as a Master Healer. It is an energy amplifier and is highly programmable, but you must dedicate your Quartz Crystal to a purpose to ensure it is amplifying the energy you want it to amplify. Wearing one in jewelry or carrying it in your pocket without setting an intention would essentially be leaving the stone to "do what it does" without guidance. If you had a stressful day, the undedicated Quartz Crystal will amplify stress. If you instead dedicate the Quartz to assist you with transmuting stressful energy, then the stone will raise your positive energetic vibration. Quartz Crystal is a unique stone because it can be asked to assist in any possible way. It can be asked to serve as a grounding stone, to increase intuition, to attract love or wealth, and to assist with communication. It is a great tool for focusing your energy and directing it toward your goals.

Intention is a powerful and often unrealized component of our overall well-being. Our words and thoughts are powerful. In hermetic philosophy, for example, the Seven Principles of the Universe include one critical concept reflected in many philosophical perspectives: *All Is Mind*. This idea is echoed in the Solipsist philosophy that only your specific mind is certain to exist. In other words, your mind is the most powerful creator in your existence and every experience you have, be it small like buying a cup of coffee or large like bearing a child, is created in the core of your specific being. It is created in your own mind by the way you choose to interpret the experience. All Is Mind; all is perspective.

At the risk of oversimplifying, if you believe something to be unhealthy, then it will manifest in your life in an unhealthy way. The opposite is also true. You tend to draw things to you that you expect to attract. The Universe will prove you right every time, because that's where your mind is focused—it will see what it expects to see. Setting an intention allows you to be open to surprises.

There is much research done on the placebo effect that suggests what we believe has a grand effect on what we physically experience. The placebo effect occurs when a person experiences positive outcomes from something which is only believed by them to help (and might not have any evidence-based helpful effect). In other words, if you take a sugar pill and *believe* it is curing your illness, it is possible that it will relieve your symptoms. Placebo effect, solipsism, and hermetic principles all describe how our minds process situations, adjust our needs, and create the skills that allow us to achieve. By believing your stone provides you with healing and wellness, you are also attuning your mind to work for you and your greatest good.

The *All Is Mind* principle can work against us as well. For example, limiting thoughts or ideas are real if you are attached to them. If you believe that success comes only from constant challenge, then your personal path to success will certainly be littered with bumps and discomfort. Likewise, if you believe relationships are out of reach or that your financial maturity can only be achieved by working ninety hours a week, then you may never reach that experience of love or financial security (or you risk not recognizing it when you do).

Often, these perceived limitations are imposed on us at a young age when we witness family members, teachers, or mentors who act from this vibration and project their beliefs onto us. The human vibration is always in a state of flux, and your energetic body is sensitive to the will of other people. Without disciplined practice, your energy can be influenced by others against your greatest good. The same goes for your thought patterns. If you grew up in a household which held a vibration of scarcity, for example, you might have come to believe that there was never enough or that everyone always has to have debt. This belief can be difficult to break, but it is essential to overcome the beliefs imposed on us by our environment. Few willingly choose to live in resource insecurity or an intentional state of limitation, and these beliefs can be challenged by crystal intention practices.

THE CRYSTAL SHIELD EXERCISE

Here is a great exercise to use your stones and crystals to discipline your energy: The Crystal Shield. To begin, complete the Intuitive Crystal Drawing Exercise and select a stone which represents you personally. Infuse that stone with the idea of your *Self* at its strongest and most resilient. Now, take your self-stone and six Quartz Crystal points. Place the self-stone on the floor or table in front of you and surround it with a circle of the six Quartz points facing outward or upward, as if they are arrows pointing outward from the center, self-stone. As you place each point, softly infuse the crystals with a mental image of protection. Tell each crystal that its job is to fend off any external energy that might cause harm to you, the stone in the center. Be sure to also tell the Quartz points that they can allow helpful energies to pass, but only if they serve your highest good and cause no harm.

Once you have placed your grid of crystals, take ten deep breaths. Really see yourself as that strong, safe, resilient, protected stone in the center. You may choose to leave this grid up for a day or a week to gather more energy. You may even choose to supplement that energy with sunlight, candlelight, moonlight, or daily prayer or intention-setting—whatever resonates with you. When you feel the work has reached its maximum potential, dismantle the grid and carry the stone that represents you in your pocket. Imagine the stone is now your personal shield, protecting you from thoughts, patterns, and energies that might disrupt your path.

There are thoughts we tend to repeat in one way or another which often solidify and hold us in a space which does not serve us. These thoughts are unique to each of us, but common patterns include: *Life is hard. Nothing lasts forever. No one understands me. I have no support. I never have enough time. I am always sick. I am cursed or unlucky. No one loves me. Everything is too expensive, and I'll never have enough money. Everything is difficult and out of reach. I cannot have what I desire, so I need to lower my expectations.* While you may experience these beliefs as inalienable truths, they are very likely *not real.* Sometimes our feelings lie to us, and how you feel is an indicator of the state of your vibration. As you say to yourself, "I can never catch a break," you may feel defeated and let down, which may create an anchor to this feeling. Remember, *All Is Mind*, so what you say to yourself is what you experience in life. When anchors of this type have been created within you, soon, situations are likely to trigger the deepest feeling of defeat even if your situation might actually be good for you.

It serves you well to be in control of what you say and think, and working with stones and using techniques like the Crystal Judge or the Crystal Shield can help you achieve better self-control over your experiences. Refuse to let a situation mess with your energy or throw you out of alignment. Choose to be in the moment, enjoy the scenery, watch the sunset, feel the wind dance through your fingertips, hear the music playing, and smell the grass or wildflowers you pass. Fundamentally, this *mindfulness* activity can jolt you out of your default vibration and shift you into the present moment. This change in perspective will release the emotion and allow you to replace it with gratitude. When you are grateful, you are attuned to an ideal vibration for manifesting wellness.

Manifesting wellness is a combination of Vibration, Intention, Focus and Discipline. Your inner thoughts and outer language must support the goals you would like to see fulfilled. To manifest wellness, speak the goal in positive language and think about the goal in terms of achievement. Imagine yourself as the person you wish to be. Your thoughts and communication are essentially data being processed by the Universe, the flow of energy, and your Subconscious Mind. Thoughts are energy that can form into action, and action leads to outcome.

You may, for example, have a statement that you repeat to yourself with a kind of self-deprecating humor. These statements, however benign you think they are, have an effect on your well-being. Lune knows a beloved soul who used to make a joke when she would forget something. "Blame it on the brain tumor," she would say. At the time, she had no reason to believe she had an actual brain tumor, but years later, she did in fact develop one and is now a survivor who takes her words and inner dialogue much more seriously. Repeating the statement "Blame it on the brain tumor," even in jest, seemed to her to have manifested in reality from her Subconscious Mind.

How often do you this? How often do you jokingly call yourself stupid, awkward, or miserable? The Subconscious Mind has no sense of humor. It takes the data you provide it and puts things into motion behind the scenes, but it is also susceptible to bias. It cannot interpret experience on its own, but it will move in whatever direction you let it. The Subconscious Mind is like a machine which can do all the heavy lifting, never gets tired, and is constantly working. The Conscious Mind, by contrast, is driving the heavy machinery.

In happiness philosophy, this is described as the Rider and the Elephant, a concept coined by Jonathan Haidt. The rider is the Conscious Mind, and it can control the direction of the Elephant (or Subconscious Mind) by engaging in an act of willpower. The Subconscious Mind is the lumbering giant that moves based on where it is directed. If you stop directing because you are overcome by emotion or projection, then the Elephant will move in whatever direction it is pushed by the energetic influences that surround you. Setting clear and focused intentions and reminding yourself about them repeatedly, such as with a crystal that you touch daily, is vital to ensuring your Rider is steering the Elephant[10].

Tending to your intentions through crystals not unlike tending to a garden. If you maintain it, it will bear fruit. If you neglect it, it will be choked out by weeds and bear nothing fruitful. Consider, for example, the work of Dr. Masaru Emoto, who performed various tests on the influence of thought and projection on water molecules. When his test subjects projected feelings and thoughts of hatred and pain onto water, the molecules of that water took on shapes which appeared disorganized and unbalanced. Conversely, when subject projected thoughts and statements of encouragement and love,

10 Jonathan Haidt, in *The Happiness Hypothesis: Finding Modern Truth in Ancient Wisdom.* Basic Books, 2006.

the molecules appeared uniform and balanced, like a snowflake or mandala.[11] Similar testing has been performed on plants, and the effects are as you would likely expect: plants which received hurtful messages shriveled and died, while plants receiving positive messages thrived. Since we are living beings like plants and comprised of water molecules, just imagine the impact your thoughts have on your body life experience. Imagine the impact that a crystal can have on your experience if you have filled it with encouraging thoughts and intentions and repeated those intentions daily.

Just as water responds to our intentions, so do gemstones, minerals, and crystals. Stones hold the vibration of your intention. Consider the act of praying over food, which has been practiced by many cultures since ancient times. Such prayer incorporates a sacred blessing and a reminder of abundance. This blessing connects a person to the experience of that food and the source of it, which is part of the interconnected web of life. Praying over crystals can have a similar effect.

Setting prayer and intention on natural objects which are connected to the bountiful Earth does not involve new practices and concepts. If you had a highly religious upbringing, you might harbor some resentment or resistance to the notion of prayer. Or, if you are an atheist, you may find that setting an intention for the highest good might conflict with some inner belief that there is no Divine Force in the Universe. At the same time, even the atheist solipsist who believes the only entity in the Universe is the singular mind she possesses must manifest her outcomes through thought and action. Working with the Subconscious Mind applies to everyone. Setting an intention may be like prayer, or it may simply be an act of cause and effect. Find what resonates with you and go from there.

---

11   Masaru Emoto, in *The Miracle of Water*. Atria Books, 2011.

CHAPTER 5

THE IMPORTANCE OF RITUALS OF RELAXATION

Rituals are routines infused by intention. They are symbolic actions that we perform in order to manifest an outcome. We've already covered in depth how important your thoughts and emotions are to your vibrational energy, as well as how that energy impacts your ability to achieve your goals. By establishing methods to alter your vibration for the better, you will be creating your safety net. When you are pushed or pulled out of comfort, you can return to the ritual— the series of actions you've infused with symbolic intention—to create, recreate, or reinforce the foundation for your own growth and progress. Ritual gets you back on your desired path when you find yourself losing your way. In this way, your intention and symbolic energy are the compass, and ritual is the map that you follow back to alignment.

Your personal rituals might change depending on the situation, but you must first impress the importance of your own awareness onto yourself and your Will in order to ensure you manifest your truth. You will need to commit to making changes in your behavior to better navigate your personal path; second only to that in importance, you will also need to develop your awareness of your own state of being. Without these two ingredients, your recipe will be unable to produce change in thought and action. Without awareness, you may be carried away by stress, anxiety, and self-doubt. Rituals with crystals can help you return to the ground.

How do you become aware of your own energy level or personal vibe? As noted, your emotions are certainly powerful signals of your vibrations, but what if you have not yet learned nonattachment? If you feel a wave of anxiety, for example, you might allow it to paint a picture of your present experience as stressful, but if you instead take an active, objective role, you can *choose* not to experience that stress by instead asking questions about the experience objectively. This is a good time to perform the Crystal Judge. You might also ask yourself these questions. *Why am I feeling this way? Am I in true danger? Is this anxious feeling telling me something, or is this a triggered emotion, perhaps from a previously established pattern? What do I choose to do with this feeling? Should I react, or shall I do what I can to move away from this feeling?*

DAILY CRYSTAL ATTUNEMENT EXERCISE

Awareness may sound like a simple achievement, but, for many, awareness will require practice and discipline. Developing a ritual for awareness is a good approach to tending the crystal garden of consciousness. Try this activity to get started. Begin each day by holding a crystal of your choosing. (You might go back to the Intuitive Crystal Drawing Exercise if you need help selecting a stone.) Now, with your gemstone in hand, set an intention to be aware of your emotional state, and acknowledge that your feelings will come up as a means of your Subconscious Mind communicating with your Conscious Mind. Tell yourself that your emotions may not necessarily be "right," but they are certainly valid. In other words, remind yourself that what you are feeling in a given moment isn't necessarily *you* even if it is what you are feeling. Set the intention into the stone that every time you touch it or gaze at it, you will be reminded of your truth. The information provided by either comfortable or uncomfortable feelings moves you closer to or further away from your ideal state of vibrational frequency. Don't judge those feelings. Just let them be what they are. Question them. Validate them. Learn from them and allow them to flow.

Perform this crystal meditation before you step out of bed. Take a few deep breaths and repeat a mantra, such as "Today I ask my Higher Self or my Subconscious Mind to bring me to a state of awareness regarding my personal state of vibration. Allow me to become fully aware of when I am both in and out of alignment with my highest goals and desires." If you are unable to set this intention before you get out of bed, then do your best to make it work for you at some point early in the day. Maybe you can keep a crystal nearby while you brush your teeth, brew your coffee, or drive to work. Remember to carry the stone or place it where you can see it throughout the day. Gemstones and minerals amplify the intention you set. It could be an intention you set while applying a few drops of essential oils to your wrists or while listening to some singing bowls' sounds in the morning. It could be something you write each day in your planner or an intention you set while watering your plants. Do this daily and focus on your gemstone to reset the intention each morning.

As you set the intention of awareness each day, you will find yourself becoming more aware. Over the course of a week or month, this awareness will intensify. Don't stop. The daily ritual will establish discipline, but only if you continue to do it even when you feel intensely aware. Research suggests three weeks or approximately twenty-one days is the length of time necessary for a daily action to become a habit. In spiritual training, such as Reiki, it has been traditionally taught that twenty-one dedicated days are needed following a session or attunement for the shift in energy to be fully processed.

Ritual works well when you use it to check in with yourself at specific times each day. For example, you might set an alarm reminder on your phone or wear a device for fitness or mindfulness that vibrates a few times a day to call your attention to the present moment. When you hear the chime or feel the vibration, tune into your stone and check in with your emotions. Picture your emotional scale as a spectrum or wheel with opposite polarities directly across from one another. If it helps, you might try assigning numbers to this scale. Across the wheel from Hate is Love, opposite Sorrow is Joy, and opposite Anxiety is Relaxation or Trust. If you can identify how you feel along this proverbial spectrum of emotional states, you can identify if that is where you want to be. If it is not a state that serves you, then take action to shift into a more comfortable state. Action can be a literal interruption, like slamming the flat of your hand against a wall and shouting "No!" It might also be an energetic interruption, like using a crystal wand to focus energy in a specific direction. Use your stone as a guidepost. Touch the stone and remind yourself of your perfect state. Choose your state and bounce back to it as you need to.

You cannot authentically move from one polar emotion to the other instantly, but you can make progress toward it. Any progress *is* progress. Acknowledging progress is critical to maintaining it. What you resist persists, but what you sustain also persists. Please don't feel like you are falling behind or tell yourself you "should" be feeling differently. Trust yourself. Use the tools and rituals you have established to move, even the slightest bit, in the vibrational direction of comfort and alignment.

The next few pages will help you create a toolbox of practices and crystals to help shift your vibration. In this toolbox, you will need both stones and other objects, as well as symbolic action or ritual. A ritual can be simple, like lifting a stone to your face and touching it to your forehead three times. Or it might be holding a stone between your palms at your heart center while you speak an intention out loud. It is the practice that will help you sustain your alignment. When you catch yourself out of alignment, open your toolbox. If you find yourself stressed out or uncomfortable, use your tools and rituals to serve your needs.

Thoughts and phrases can also find a place in your toolbox. Some people decorate a container, like an old cigar box or tea tin, with a collage and paint and fill it with crystals and affirmations. Affirmations, when read or said aloud, become thoughts and phrases we can use to shift our energy. You might include: *I understand that I am in control of my life and my direction. I choose to actively participate, and therefore I take responsibility for my thoughts, actions, and reactions. I validate my current emotions and sensations, and I hereby release them. I trust my intuition. I choose to use my practices to help me feel calmer and shift into relaxation.*

Consider what you yourself find uniquely relaxing. What works for others, like hot sudsy baths, may not work for you. That's okay. If you are the type who feels truly relaxed and at peace while hiking in the woods, then what can you do to relax when you are at your place of business in the city? Perhaps your job allows you to take a break and you're able to walk around the block or at least step outside for some fresh air, but what if you are on a plane or otherwise unable to step outside and move? This is why we are all best served by having a toolbox of rituals, affirmations, and stones.

DEVELOPING YOUR TOOLBOX:

Validation and Awareness: Hold a stone of your choosing in your hands at heart center. Take three cleansing breaths. Bring your awareness to how you are feeling. Now, without judging how you feel, validate those emotions, and sit with them for a moment. You are feeling them because they are valid responses to your situation, but you need not give in to them. Completely feel them, even if they are uncomfortable. Please note that if you are dealing with mental illness, you may want to seek guidance from a qualified counselor to assist you with this process.

Assess the situation and notice where you are on an emotional scale. Do your best to remove yourself from identifying with any feelings of discomfort and expand your perspective to identify the cause of your feelings. Is the feeling merited? Is it a signal for you to take an action or make a choice? Or is this an internal issue for you to address personally?

For example, jealousy is a common, uncomfortable feeling which may require your attention and discernment. If you are feeling jealous in a relationship, bring your awareness to the feeling, name it, and validate it. Why do you feel this way? Where in your body do you feel it? What do you think is causing you to feel it? Has your partner betrayed your committed arrangement? Or is this coming from some other source? If you have not been betrayed, then this ritual will help you experience honest self-reflection. Perhaps you will find that your partner is trusting and supportive and your own jealousy is brought about by an unrelated past experience. Ask the stone to help you release this unrelated experience. Forgive yourself and your partner or friend. Express your gratitude. Release three more cleansing breaths, and then return the stone to its place.

~~~~~~

Breath: Breath work is one of the most helpful tools for wellness because you can always focus on your breath to bring yourself back to the present moment. Breathing affects your mental state, and, in yogic practices, there are a variety of methods you can employ to engage different breath work outcomes. For instance, you can use the "fire breath" technique by rapidly breathing in and out to generate heat, or you can cool yourself by rolling your tongue and breathing through it. However you breathe, just begin monitoring your breathing. Don't try to alter it. Just observe it. Pay attention to the gentle ebb and flow of your lungs. Feel your stomach and chest rise with each inhale and sink with each exhale.

Another exercise is to control the breath. This is a yogic method called *Pranic Breathing*, which is taught within Kundalini Yoga. Pranic Breathing requires you to use your attention to change the pattern of breath and shift your state of consciousness. It draws on the energetic body and helps you to alter your vibration through specific breath work. Though Pranic Breathing does create positive change, simply becoming aware of your breath or slowing and deepening its rhythm are effective methods for relaxation and vibrational stability. Please do not attempt the following Pranic Breathing exercise without first checking with your medical practitioner if you have any medical issue which could be worsened by altered breathing, such as a history of stroke or asthma. Additionally, listen to your body and take a gentle approach to breath work.

To begin, sit comfortably in an aligned posture and become aware of your breathing. Is it shallow? Are you holding your breath? Inhale through your nostrils a deliberate, deep, and comfortable breath to a count of six if you are just starting out with this practice. As you progress in your skill, you may increase this number gradually to eight, ten, and so on. Hold your inhalation for half the time it took you to inhale. For example, if you inhaled for six seconds, now hold your breath for three. Then, exhale through your mouth for the same amount of time you inhaled. Hold your breath again for half the time of your exhale. Again, listen to your body and do not overdo it. If you are a beginner, start with just a few breaths in this pattern and choose a count that is comfortable for you, whether that is six seconds as suggested or four seconds or eight. The point is to be aware of what works for you and to honor that process.

The important thing here is to deepen and slow your breath to a pace and rhythm that is more relaxed than what you observed when you first started this exercise. Be aware and deliberate. Through this shift in breath, you are taking more oxygen into your system, and this can cause you to feel a bit lightheaded or tingly. This is why it is typically suggested to perform Pranic breath work while seated comfortably. These are many resources for studying and practicing Pranic Breathing and the benefits it has for the body, mind, and spirit.

~~~~~~

Visualization: As you breathe deeply and slowly, visualize inhaling vital energy into your entire body, and, as you exhale, visualize tension, stress, and discomfort being released and recycled. Blue can be a calming and relaxing color, so it may help to picture blue tinted light or a waterfall of blue washing over your energetic body through your breath. Red is a color of vitality and physical wellness, so if you are feeling run down or under the weather, imagine a brilliant ruby-colored light instead. For mental clarity and balanced discernment, you might visualize golden yellow. The colors mentioned here are also the three primary colors, and, just as when mixing paints, we are able to blend and create our own color choices based on the basic principles related to these three primaries. Thus, merging calm-blue with clarity-yellow creates discerning-love-green. Or relaxing-blue and upbeat-red create intuitively-aligned-purple.

Another way to use visualization to enhance your overall vibration is to imagine your "mental movie." This is a great visualization to imprint on a Quartz point. Take three cleansing breaths. Now, imagine a movie projecting from the crystal to a screen in your mind. Play yourself a movie that includes you in a situation you wish to experience which is beautiful, inspiring, and comforting. Really see this movie play out for as long as you need. When you have completed the image in your mind, watch the "end credits," which express gratitude to all the resources that made the movie possible, such as your job, family, or nutritional choices. Then return to the present and take the Quartz "projector" to a place where you will see it regularly. Whenever you look at it, remember your movie.

CHAPTER 6

CHAKRA WELLNESS

As we previously noted, the chakra system provides us with a great template for where and how to focus our crystal and stone healing work. Perhaps the most familiar chakra system relates Kundalini, the ancient Indian Tantric explanation for the energy body, which is often conceptualized in this practice as a snake coiled in the pelvis that spirals up the spine through the crown of the head. It is also described as light passing through a prism—or a *crystal*—which refracts that light into all the colors of a rainbow. The traditional Hatha Yoga and Tantric Hindu systems do not isolate just seven primary chakras, but Western tradition and the simplicity of the rainbow give us a great place to focus our energy as we align crystals with our energetic needs.

The term chakra itself means "wheel," and it can be helpful to imagine wheels spinning one atop the next like gears stacked on a gear shaft, with each one in a color of the rainbow. These are energetic portals or vortices between the physical and subtle bodies. While there are countless actual energy wheels in the body, it is possible to really home in on seven major themes of energy in our bodies; most Westerners come to understand these as the Crown, Third Eye, Throat, Heart, Solar Plexus, Sacral, and Root centers. Each of these energy points is associated with a theme, and you can focus your healing by attuning to each of these chakras to address personal discord or imbalance, improve your resonance with the universal life forces, and identify your needs for overall wellness.

While this book focuses on the seven rainbow chakras, note that there are other chakra systems, including the Hara, Native American, and Tibetan chakra systems. There are also other areas of esoteric study, such as Gnosticism or Chinese medicine, which align energetic work with different anatomical parts of the body. But in the Western world, the seven primary chakras of the Kundalini system are certainly the

most commonly recognized. When you learn to read these points as
either balanced, over-energized, or under-energized, you will learn to
identify where you can focus your crystal and stone healing work.

GENERAL ASSOCIATIONS OF THE SEVEN PRIMARY CHAKRAS

Crown (Sahasrara, or "thousand-petaled [flower]"):
Top of head near fontanelle.
Color: Purple, Violet, White
Associations: Spiritual Connection, Meditation, Higher Realms
Crystal Language: "I imagine."

Third Eye (Ajna, or "command"):
Middle of forehead
Color: Indigo, Deep Purple, Dark Blue
Associations: Intuition, Inspiration, Visualization, Creative Thinking
Crystal Language: "I see."

Throat (Vishuddha, or "special and pure"):
Base of neck near clavicle bones
Color: Blue
Associations: Expression, Thought, Logic and Intellect
Crystal Language: "I express."

Heart (Anahata, or "unstruck" or "unmoving"):
Center of chest near anatomical heart
Color: Green
Associations: Love, Soul's Desires, Life Purpose
Crystal Language: "I love."

Solar Plexus (Manipura, or "jeweled metropolis"):
Upper abdomen just below ribs
Color: Yellow
Associations: Action, Authenticity, Personal Power
Crystal Language: "I create."

Sacral (Svadhisthana, or "where the self resides"):
Lower abdomen three finger widths below belly button
Color: Orange
Associations: Emotions, Creative Energy, Relationships
Crystal Language: "I feel."

Root (Muladhara, or "root" like a tree root):
Bottom of torso
Color: Red
Associations: Physical Needs, Safety, Earth Realm Connection
Crystal Language: "I am."

While many texts have been written on the subject of chakras, we speak to you from personal experience as spiritual and healing practitioners sharing with you what we have witnessed and learned through personal healing and development. Much of what we've come to understand about chakra and crystal energy healing is knowledge we have acquired through hundreds of energy healing sessions with clients. The colors of each chakra help us to identify colorful stones to use in our wellness practices, but it can also be useful to think of each chakra as a vibration or sound. Each chakra resonates at its own frequency, and, while some of us might be better at *visualizing* an area that needs our light, others may need to *hear* the places within the self that are calling out for crystal healing.

Truthfully, the chakras are not universally experienced as colors, sounds, or sensations. Some practitioners may intuit mental pictures for each of the chakra zones, images which may play out like scenes of a movie or bring about physical body sensations. Some people taste them, others smell them, and still others have no association with them at all but manipulate the area by touch like a massage therapist. They may feel the energy as if they are inching fingers along the edge of the wall to find the light switch when the power goes out.

PENDULUM DOWSING EXERCISE

Another great strategy for sensing a misaligned chakra is pendulum dowsing. Suspend either a crystal or another weight such as a ring from any string and hold it loosely over or in front of your body in alignment with the chakra points. Allow yourself to be still after grounding and centering. Then ask the pendulum to show you a "yes."; notice this movement, such as clockwise, counterclockwise, forward and backward, or side to side. Next ask it to show you a "no," again taking note of the style of the swing so you are able to identify your unique yes and no pendulum responses. Begin at the Crown and ask, "Is my Crown Chakra balanced?" Observe the response. Should you witness a no response, ask, "Is my Crown Chakra hyper-energized?" If the response is again no, ask, "Is my chakra under-energized?" Then move to the Third Eye and the other following chakras with the same practice. We would suggest keeping a journal of your chakra readings, recording the states so you may easily reflect on your readings and develop deeper comprehension of the chakra states.

STONE-ENERGY JAR ACTIVITY

Another excellent way to start aligning with the chakras is to create a Stone-Energy Jar. Begin by searching a natural area where you can find and retrieve rocks that feel right to you. Please note that most national parks do not allow you to remove stones from the area, but many outdoor places don't mind if you grab a stone from the water's edge or from alongside the path where you are walking. Just be sure to check ahead of time to make sure you know the rules. Try to find seven stones that fit easily in your pockets. Set the stones in the sunlight for a day to "clear" them while you work on your jar. You can use any old glass jar you have lying around; even old peanut butter jars work beautifully. You will be placing your stones inside this jar, so you may choose something transparent so you can see the hopes with which you fill it, or you may elect to decoupage the outside with strips of torn tissue paper or magazine clippings.

Once you are satisfied with your jar, grab a permanent magic marker and retrieve your stones. Now, focusing on each of your chakras one at a time, write a short word or message on the stone that aligns with your idea of what a positive, balanced chakra might express. If you are stuck, you might choose to use the "crystal language" phrases we listed above. One at a time, hold the stone close to your chakra point and say, "I feel balanced and well when I think of this chakra." Also speak aloud the phrase or word you wrote on your stone, and then place that stone in the jar. The next time you feel out of alignment or just want to meditate on your personal energy, reach into the jar and intuitively select any of the stones. Read the phrase you wrote on it and, while holding it in your hands, breathe your energy into the stone as you settle the energy of that chakra in your mind.

As with all language and symbol systems, it is common to find discrepancies in the description of the seven primary chakras and

their states—they are, after all, thousands of years old, having
made their first documented appearance in Vedic texts sometime
around 1500 BCE. The first English translations of the Hindu Vedas
appeared around the height of the alchemical movements of the
Renaissance, which is ironic when you consider this was also a time
when, in much of the Western world, even hinting at non-Christian
religious texts could get you hanged or burned as a witch or heretic.
These translations most often refer to the chakra as a "wheel," but it
has also been translated as "portal," which is decidedly different than
wheel—one opens like a door and transports you from one place to
another, and the other spins in a machine to grind flour or move a
vehicle around. We often hear of "opening" up our chakras, but the
word "open" might be a little misleading. A constantly "open chakra"
might make you feel like you are walking around in the dead of
winter with an "open" coat. After a while, you'd pull all that cold into
your body and start to ache.

The process of developing one's chakras is one of dedication to the
spiritual life and discipline. For example, a person with a dedicated,
open Heart Chakra would rather die than hurt another living
being, but what happens when you need to defend yourself or when
an insect smashes into your windshield while you're out driving?
Similarly, if you had a constantly open Third Eye, you would always
be catching premonitions of the future or past instead of living in
the present moment. Those who reach these levels of activation are
typically so committed to the development of their spiritual nature
in physical embodiment that they've learned to tolerate that level
of having a constantly open door to the energetic self. An average
person might tolerate a chakra that briefly opened, but typically this
experience is overwhelming and not sustainable.

Ultimately, we want to use our stones to help us ground and center
into a state of balance. You want to adjust both hyperactive and
hypoactive energies to remain attuned to your "window" of tolerance.

In other words, everyone has a window of tolerance for the world around them. This can be experienced particularly during times of distress, and you might rise above or fall below that window. The goal is to find the sweet spot where you can tolerate both distress and joy while still feeling your feelings, living your healthy life, and experiencing success. Here's a brief summary of the three primary chakra states:

BALANCED

A balanced chakra is one existing in comfort, flow, harmony, and communication. It is functioning optimally for your purposes and is your ideal state for that energetic theme. When in doubt, Quartz Crystal is a generalist which amplifies any chakra, but be careful not to use one when your chakra is over-energized, as it may just hyperactivate you. A good stone for general balance in this case would be Hematite or a darkly colored Agate. You need to be balanced to manifest your heart's desires and move in ways that are empowered and in alignment with your wishes.

UNDER-ENERGIZED

An under-energized chakra moves slowly or has an energy blockage. In this state, the chakra is not in alignment and is not supporting your highest good. Depending on the specific chakra zone, an under-energized or blocked point will manifest in different ways. You might find you have trouble hearing the messages of your soul, or you may feel isolated, fearful, passionless, and blocked. You might also feel disconnected from others and repressed. In general, any stone in the same color as the chakra you are experiencing as under-energized will help raise that energy. In the case of the Heart Chakra, you may use either green (the traditional color) or vibrant pink stones to raise the vibrational energy of that portal.

OVER-ENERGIZED

An over-energized chakra is also out of alignment with the desires of the soul and creates discord and discomfort. It may feel like energies are manic and moving too quickly, as if the theme of the chakra is spiraling out of control and away from the major focus of your present life. Depending on the chakra, over-energized portals can manifest as confusion, racing thoughts, paranoia, poor personal boundaries, excessive ego, manic emotional states, and rage. It can help to choose a stone that balances its "opposite" or "anchor" chakra. For example, if your Crown Chakra is over-energized, you might want to work with red stones to pull the energy down from your Crown into your Root (the Crown's anchor). If your Third Eye is hyperactive, you might use orange stones to pull that energy into its Sacral anchor, and so on.

ACTIVATED

Chakra activation does not equate to the "open" chakras about which we previously warned. When your chakra is activated, its energetic theme is on the surface and easily accessible to you. Your abilities related to that theme will be more obvious. When you experience a chakra awakening, you might experience increased intuition or spiritual connection. You might be able to process love and forgiveness without judgment or attachment. You might have an awakening of one chakra point many times in your life, each time enhancing the point more expansively. In the example of the Third Eye, the first activation might enhance dream states like lucid dreaming, while future activations might develop clairvoyance. Chakras can continue to develop throughout your lifetime. The chakra activation process can be anchored in stones we carry or wear. Not only do these stones remind us of the energy intentions we have for that chakra, it also can help us reactivate them when we need to reground or center.

OPEN

A truly open chakra is most commonly developed through extreme discipline, application, and focus, as well as dedication to the vibration of love and well-being. Types of people who are able to function with open chakras might be monks, yogis, or other spiritual leaders dedicated to this practice. While we do not wish to impose any limitations on you, in our experience, an opened chakra is achieved through much personal development and ascension. While any stone can help to hold a chakra open, Quartz Crystal is ideal for amplifying the open state.

Checking your own or another's chakra points can provide clarity. It can help identify where best to focus as the person "reading" the chakra will begin to pick up on patterns the chakras communicate with one another. It is very common that an energy reading will reveal an area that is out of alignment and serve as a guide to redirect your personal energy to another chakra in order to address the issue.

Very often in your healing practice, you will identify an area you believe to be out of balance and discover upon careful examination that it is the chakra above or below the misaligned one which is causing that imbalance. For example, if you feel disconnected from your creative energy and unable to "birth" new projects or complete creative tasks, you might with good reason assume your Sacral Chakra is imbalanced. But when checking these portals, you may very well find that the Sacral is in perfect balance while the chakra associated with expression, the Throat, is the one that is under-

energized, preventing you from expressing your creative energy. With
this understanding, shift your focus from trying to build creative
energy in the Sacral Chakra to instead balancing your expression
in the Throat Chakra so that your creative ideas can flow more
abundantly. Remember the general rule about crystal healing when
you tune into your chakras: Amplify with Quartz, energize with color
which vibrates at the same frequency you wish to augment, and tame
with the opposite color frequency to subdue the energy of the chakra
you are working.

Sometimes, though, you may not be aware of your chakra's energy
state, and, because this excess energy causes noticeable imbalances in
your life, you will continue with disruptive practices which keep you
out of alignment. The Heart Chakra, where all your love is nurtured,
is a good example of this. It might seem paradoxical that you could
be too loving, but it is possible to give too much of yourself without
reciprocation. You might have a hard time saying "no" or maintaining
healthy boundaries. If you give too much love outwardly, you will
eventually burn out. In a hyperactive Heart state, you may attract the
love of people who take much and give little in return.

While no situation is black and white, there are common guidelines
you can follow as you begin to understand your energetic nature and
how that energy dances with the energy of those around you. Crystal
healing can amplify your attraction in any direction, whether that is
toward more or less of what you need. The chakras serve as a guide to
manifesting wellness and personal growth. They can help you uncover
repressed issues to make space for the qualities, relationships, careers,
and experiences you desire.

As you practice your chakra sensations and hone your crystal healing
abilities, you will come to identify the ways your chakras support
your heart's calling, which are your greatest goals and manifestations.
There is no limit to these goals, but there are limiting thoughts and

choices. The chakras are guides to understanding where you might be affected by self-limiting beliefs which may hold you in a state of stagnation. By identifying imbalanced chakras, you can learn to stop "spinning your wheels" and create new patterns which support your desires. Stones can work like keys to unlock new, expansive thoughts which do not limit you.

CRYSTAL AFFIRMATION ACTIVITY

Use your stones as part of a self-written ritual using positive self-talk and association. Instead of saying, "I don't have enough time," you might use a yellow stone for the Solar Plexus Chakra, which manifests our sense of time. Breathe into it a solution-focused, positive message, such as, "I can spend my time best by prioritizing the following values," and then fill in the blanks. What do you value most? How do you want to prioritize your time? Now, you have a stone that can remind you of your positive self-message. Every time you hold it or look at it, whisper your new positive phrase to yourself and take three cleansing breaths. If you don't know your values, take it back another step and use a green stone to ask your Heart Chakra about your life purpose, or take it down to the Root with a red stone to ask that your need for security is met. To find your values, ask yourself: *What is my life purpose? How can I discover my life path? Where in this world and in my life am I given the free will to create my own path? Where am I experiencing friction or unhappiness?*

CENTERING ON THE HEART

When we first began this energy healing research years ago, we would have stated that no chakra is more important than the next. While it is still true that we hold with this belief, we have witnessed that it is the message of the Heart that the other chakras must learn to hear and effectively support. As the center of the energy path, the Heart functions as a kind of generator for the house that is your body. It's a bit like the Four Corners in the southwestern United States or any other crossroads where multiple roads meet: Energy travels up from the Heart to the Crown and back down again, just as it travels down from the Heart to the Root and back up again, but it is the Heart that manifests all our greatest works. It is the place of true discernment, and it is one of two places in the energetic body which directly accesses the soul (the other is the Third Eye, or Pineal Gland).

The Heart is essentially the brain of the soul. It has an innate knowledge of what we have come into this lifetime to experience, and it guides you best by helping you to feel good. Ever cross paths with a person on the street and have an instant liking for them? That's probably your Heart telling you to say hello. Ever encounter someone who gives you the creeps? That is probably also your Heart telling you to run for the hills! Your Heart recognizes the vibration of love and kindness—both what you are called to give as well as what you deserve to receive. It calls you to become a parent, create art, build businesses, travel, and fall in love so that you may learn more about yourself and develop in ways that are impossible without community. It also teaches you how to love yourself and how you may gain a sense of completion from life. When your Heart is aligned, you recognize your purpose. You are here in your body on this planet to achieve personal fulfillment, and your Heart Chakra is the guide to that purpose.

CRYSTAL WORTHINESS MEDITATION

Crystal Worthiness Meditation: A simple crystal healing practice for your Heart Chakra begins with a piece of Rose Quartz (or, indeed, any stone that speaks to you. We're fans of heart-shaped Labradorite, with its flashes of green or often multicolored light!). Hold the stone in your dominant hand and close your palm around it. Now place your left palm flat against your Heart and tune into the sensation of your heartbeat. You may find it easier to close your eyes while you do this to quiet the other senses and focus on your center. Once you feel its steady thumping within your chest, bring your hand with the stone up and place it over your nondominant hand so they are stacked with the stone between them. Now breathe into your Heart by imagining that area of your body filling with a bright, lush, mossy green swell of air. As you exhale, whisper aloud, "I love myself. I forgive myself. I have compassion for myself. I deserve love. I am worthy." Repeat this meditation daily, and keep your stone in a place where you can gaze at it throughout the day, like on your desk or nightstand. If you want, you can even use it in the Chakra Map you will be developing later in this chapter.

Remember as you tune into your heart that there is no "good" or "bad" emotional response. Feelings crop up in heart-healing work in vivid ways, but emotions themselves are neither right nor wrong, even if you assign these labels to them. When someone you love dies, for example, it is natural and perhaps even best to experience the grief of that death, just as it is natural to experience joy when you reach creative flow doing something you love to do. Navigating your personal path begins by connecting to your Heart's desires. Your goals are not complete destinations unless they also include the emotional state you wish to experience. If the feeling of peace and happiness is not included in your desires, then you might achieve those goals but remain unfulfilled or at least deplete your energy as you try to manifest them.

Tune into your Heart to perceive the many choices available to you—those sudden opportunities that crop up each day. When you know what you *want to feel* in addition to what you *want to have*, you are changing your perspective. It's a bit like shining a flashlight down a dark corridor. If you always shine it up, you'll only ever see the ceiling. As soon as you refocus where the light shines (perhaps the floor), you become *able* to see different things you missed before, like the ring misplaced last week or the toy your child dropped and wailed about all night before bed. Aligning your emotions with your actions through intention and by imagining how they *will feel and be* is the secret to manifesting wellness.

Because the Heart is the central point for your energetic work, in which you bring together your sense of both Heaven and Earth, it might be helpful to discover just how our Heart Chakra communicates, right? The Heart Chakra Rose Quartz affirmation is helpful, but what about when you just can't bring yourself to hear or even say the words? How can you hear your Heart in order to be guided to your goals? The Heart doesn't always speak clearly. It is certainly possible to "hear" what your goal is, but sometimes you might be out of touch with that zone and need to reestablish your rapport with your Heart to truly hear what it has to say.

Think back on the Stone-Energy Jar activity where you filled a jar with stones, each inscribed with a chakra affirmation. One way the Heart might communicate indirectly is dowsing within your jar. Reach intuitively into your jar and pull out a stone. What is its message for you? Or perhaps you see a set of numbers repeating on your clock or you keep waking from a dream you can't remember even though you know it must be important. When you experience that sensation of the unexpected, lean into it. Tune in. Could it be your Heart trying to redirect your attention?

Trust the messages you receive from your Heart, even if they don't exactly make sense to you. Ever go through a rough patch right before experiencing something delightful? Perhaps you were laid off from a job and then found your dream job a month later by happenstance? It stinks while you're going through the layoff, but then when you get that dream job, you walk on air. In the moment the layoff happens, you're in the quagmire of grief (which, remember, isn't "bad," even if you want to label it that way. It's okay to grieve). A few months later, you are in the clouds of joy. It is only through zooming out of the experience and taking a bird's-eye view of the path that led to your dream job that you can see what steps led you there, even if at the time it stank. Similar to stepping-stones crossing a stream, one footfall leads to the next to get you back on track to your desires.

Take this example of the way your Heart can show you your path. There was a woman who was grieving deeply after the passing of her son. What a horrible and devastating experience it is to suddenly find yourself in a world without your child whom you carried in your body and loved to the core of your Heart. She kept having this squiggly message in the back of her mind that she needed to get a massage, but this confused her. She was, after all, grieving, and sometimes people put self-care on the back burner when handling the weight of despair. She wasn't one to get massages, but one day she found herself walking down a street near her home where she passed a building with a sign out front for a licensed massage therapist. Something compelled her to go inside. When she shared the story of her son's passing with the therapist, the therapist mentioned that in another office in the same building, there was a spiritual guide who hosted afterlife events. This same grieving mother, who had been reticent about getting a massage, followed one stepping-stone to the next to that spiritual guide and discovered there a group of people who had gone through similar grief experiences. Because she listened to her Heart telling her to get a massage, she took one step after another until she found a supportive community of other grieving parents. It was an indirect message, but she listened and found what she needed to grow and survive in the wake of a terrible life tragedy. Unfortunately, you know in your Heart that you cannot avoid a tragedy like death. Sorrow and grief are emotions most will face in a lifetime. Radical acceptance and listening to the Heart's healing perspective can help you cope.

The Heart is your emotional brain and is linked directly to your sense of fulfillment and purpose. The Root is linked to the physical demands of that Heart's desire, such as outer body health or the resources available to achieve it. The Sacral Chakra is tied to your personal connections to those who might support your desire, as well as to your emotional compass about the world around you. The Solar Plexus supports the Heart's desire by helping you to act, shift how you see yourself, and experience authenticity. Moving above the Heart now, the healthy Throat Chakra expresses your emotional desires in clear and articulate ways, both internally and externally. The Third Eye is where you visualize these Heart goals and see yourself comfortably achieving them. Finally, the Crown is your connection to the unseen and how your Heart's desire supports and is supported by the greater community around you—when you achieve happiness, you bring that happiness to others, too. The Heart is the engine that drives it all. If you are just starting your stone collection, choose stones that resonate foremost with your Heart, and if you already have a collection, add to it stones that help you feel love. Put your Heart into it and listen to what it tells you is right.

CREATING YOUR CHAKRA MAP

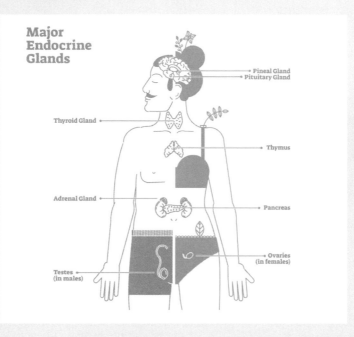

Focus your crystal healing practice and synthesize your chakra understanding by creating a Chakra Crystal Map. There are lots of different ways you can conceptualize your map—sculpture, drawing, collage, and mixed media. Whatever way you choose to create your energy map, we encourage you to incorporate stones into it to help you get a feel for what stones you feel align best with each chakra so you can more easily select the ones you need when the moment arises. Since the chakra system travels along the spine like a path, what better way to understand the flow of that energy than by creating a map? And what better place to start than with the Heart?

To begin your map, get yourself a cluster of seven stones that you feel each resonate with one of your chakras. These might be flat-backed stones so you can work them into a two-dimensional map, like a drawing or mixed media collage. They might be river stones that you paint the colors of the rainbow or, as with the Stone-Energy Jar, cover with written affirmations. You might even head to the craft store and grab yourself some crystal chips, which are tiny, fingernail-sized stones similar to gravel. Once you have your materials, you're ready to plot your crystal Chakra Map.

Sculpture: Make a basic human figure out of natural, air-drying clay. Before the clay dries fully, press the stones into it where they align with the chakra points. You might press an Amethyst point into the top of the head, for instance, and a chip of Chrysoprase into the Heart Center. Or start with the heart and work your way up and down. The goal here is to get a psychomotor connection (or a body connection) to the locations of the chakras in three dimensions. This will help you as you learn where to find them in your own body.

Crystal Chips: Draw or print a human figure onto paper. Fill a chakra-sized section of the figure with glue, and sprinkle stone chips onto the glue-pile so it fills the space. Continue this way until you've filled the figure with crystal chips from pelvis to head in a full rainbow. You may want to move the chips around with the palm of your hand or the back of a wooden spoon until they land in configurations that fit your vision.

Stone Collage: Take a piece of heavy cardstock or corrugated cardboard. Select stones with a flat back, and use glue to affix them in a rainbow with red at the bottom and purple at the top. For this example, you may or may not choose to work with a human figure. The goal is to get the stones in the chakra sequence you'll be working with and to get a feel for what stones resonate in each space of the chakra spine. In this example and the crystal-chip example above, you might consider using a marker to jot down the name of the chakra and any notes about the energy theme and stones you relate to it.

Impermanent Mandala Grid: A crystal grid is a very simple stone map you can make that you can change all the time if you like. Using crystals, shells, twigs, acorns, magazine cut-outs, or anything else that speaks to you about the chakras, arrange them on a countertop or tabletop in a pleasing pattern. Ground and center as you arrange the pieces so the pattern formed is both meditative and intuitive. Whatever you design in this grid isn't permanent—you can change it multiple times a day, if you want to. Just think about the chakras and the stones that you feel match them as you arrange your mandala before you.

Crystal-Pendulum Chain: Select crystal beads in the colors of the rainbow with a bead-druzy or pendant for the end of the chain. Using jump rings and a pair of needle-nosed pliers, start by connecting the pendant of your pendulum to a ring. Fasten a second ring to the first and link a red stone bead. Continue up the chain until you reach the purple Crown bead. Finish with a "handle," which might be another crystal-bead that is just a little smaller than the pendant or a small metal rod. Fasten the handle to the rest of the chain and practice dowsing your chakras with it.

Whichever Crystal Map process you choose, we also recommend you write a compass or "guide" for your map in a journal. Keep notes about which stones resonate with you for each chakra. Jot down a few ideas as to why you think so. Is it the color? The shape? Is it where and how you found the stone or a memory about how the stone showed up in your life? Reflect on the connection you have to your stones. Keep track of which stones draw you for which energetic purposes and how they relate to your chakras. It can also be helpful to track which comes first: is it an awareness of the chakra that compels you to find a stone, or is it intuitively picking up a stone that helps you realize which chakra needs your attention? The more you attend to your inner self and tune into your energetic body, the easier it will be to keep track of the chakras and the stones that appeal to these vibrations.

CHAPTER 7

CHAKRAS, ENERGY PATHWAYS, AND CRYSTALS

There are different schools of thought on the chakra system. In some schools, there are thousands—perhaps even an infinite number—of chakras in the body, each aligned to a different purpose. In most Western traditions, though, the chakras tend to be synthesized to just seven or nine centralized chakra themes that correspond to the colors of the rainbow, and, therefore, a stone's color can then be used to easily identify which chakra it is likely to support.

If your chakras are in balance, then you are probably feeling a general sense of well-being. An over-energized chakra is hyperfocused on itself and sends out and takes in the energy of its theme at a higher rate than it should. An under-energized chakra is sluggish and sometimes doesn't even accept or transmit that energy at all. Imagine that a chakra is like a pottery wheel. When things are going well, the wheel is spinning evenly and you can mold the clay into a symmetrical bowl that will one day hold water. If the wheel is over-energized, it's spinning too fast and the clay flings itself off the wheel and spatters the wall. It can no longer hold its intended shape. And if the wheel is under-energized, it isn't spinning fast enough for you to do anything but look at the lump of clay in the middle. The way we use stones or energy to harmonize a chakra imbalance differs only slightly based on the speed that the wheel is spinning; sometimes the speed influences which stone we might choose to generate balance.

Chakras also do not work in isolation; achieving balance in one area with one stone might rely on working with another area with another stone as well. In this respect, the pottery wheel analogy needs to be expanded to perhaps an axle on which several wheels are spinning, one atop the other and in multiple directions. If, say, your Heart Chakra is over-energized, it might be that your Throat Chakra is also over-energized and your Solar Plexus Chakra is sluggish and not letting the heart "vent." If one wheel on this imaginary axle is spinning quickly, it might be causing friction on the wheel below it, causing that one to spin slower. In this situation, you might need to bring in one stone for the slow wheel to get it to speed up a bit and another for the fast wheel to calm it. To expand this mental image further, you might apply it to your own body, where the axle is the spine and the wheels start around your pelvis and follow your spine up to just above your head. Imagine where you might hold, hover, or place stones against your body to get those wheels spinning in a direction and at a speed that serves your greatest good.

Tune into where your chakra energy might benefit from some crystal meditation and attention. Remember that chakras are always moving even when they are moving very slowly. This is important to remember because a chakra is never static; it can change at any given time, and, for this reason, it can be helpful to have many different stones in your collection that you attune and prepare for the different states of each of your chakras. More often than not, you will find there is a "big picture" theme you can apply to your current circumstance, and that can help you decide which crystals to use and how you might refocus your energy to serve your needs.

CROWN STATES

The Crown Chakra is located at the very top of the head and just above it. It is typically represented by either a rich purple or a white or clear color, so stones like Amethyst, Sugilite, and Selenite are often used when working with this space.

Balanced Crown

When the Crown Chakra is balanced, you will feel a healthy connection to what lies beyond the physical world and to your sense of spirituality. You will feel like you are connected to the invisible and the divine—to the world that isn't seen. You may see or communicate with Spirit, God, Goddess, the Universe, the Higher Self, Angels, ancestors, spirit guides, or even just the higher mind and inner self. Prayer and meditation come easily when the Crown is in balance, and you may embrace the oneness of humanity and the knowledge that we are all doing our best. You will likely feel self-aware and connected to *all that is*.

Because the Crown can be visualized as a purple or white light that starts just *above your head*, you can also imagine a balanced Crown as your moving connection to everything above you. When balanced, you may even experience a kind of "lift" upward from the Crown, as if you are becoming lighter or being pulled up by a kite string. In fact, when your Crown is balanced and working well, you might even find you sit up straighter or have better walking posture as your upward energy seems to draw you up. You may also feel receptive to messages that come "down" to you from above (such as from the realm of thoughts, the air, the sky, or whatever you may imagine as divine or heavenly). To amplify your sense of balance, use Clear Quartz Crystal points or purple stones like Charoite to hold this level state for yourself.

Core Issue for Crown Imbalance

When the Crown Chakra is imbalanced, the root of the issue is an inability to connect with your highest Self, God or Goddess, divinity, or the Universe. It boils down to your overall sense of trust. There is an element of hope or faith in the importance of your life experience nestled in this Crown Chakra, a trust that your Heart's desires can and will be fulfilled and that you are supported by not only your own actions and discipline, but also in ways that are unseen.

Remember that your life is not in isolation but is connected to a cosmic web of which we are all a part. We contribute to cause and effect; we "add the good" through every action and thought we create. Since stones existed long before us and will likely carry on long after we are gone, it can be helpful in general service to our Crown Chakras to remember that whatever stones we are using have a sense of *permanence* to them. They are *of the Earth*, and therefore represent the body and the ground beneath us.

Over-Energized Crown

An over-energized Crown Chakra may indicate an unease connecting with the Earth and other things we consider "worldly," like eating, connecting with family or friends, or developing lifestyle routines. You might be using meditation to experience the out-of-body forms of avoidance or escape. Because the Crown is where your energy both leaves and enters the body at the top of that "axle," an over-energized Crown typically means you are spending too much of your energy in the air and not enough in the body. In other words, you're trying to disassociate from your physical body and sensory experiences. In extreme cases, an over-energized crown could be an indication of wanting to be done with the Earthly experience or perhaps even contemplating suicide. Substance use and other forms of self-medicating in order to disconnect from the body can also occur when the Crown is hyper-energized.

You might experience migraines, anxiety, insomnia, or dizziness. You may also be feeling overwhelmed yet detached at the same time or generally spaced out. You might also have difficulty understanding the nature of the world and find yourself dwelling on world issues, like politics, religion, or human suffering without finding a way to self-actualize. It is as though the world is overwhelming to you and you don't feel your own sense of agency. If you find you are experiencing an over-energized crown, you may find you are having an expansive spiritual or universal connection but may not be adequately grounding the energy, like a bolt of lightning hitting a house without a lightning rod.

To balance an over-energized Crown Chakra, ground and center. Embrace the things you associate with the earthly realm. Eat a good meal and do something physically active, like jogging around the block or performing a yoga asana. You can also connect to your physical senses by dancing or drumming or connect to the Earth by planting or caring for a kitchen herb. Remember that you are here and now in this time and space. For some of you, this might mean being an advocate or activist for social and political change, but, for many, it is more about remembering that you possess a unique vibration. Simply being "you" is divine, and your presence here has an impact on the energy of the entire Earth in some way.

Because an over-energized Crown likely means an under-energized root, consider looking at the Root Chakra section for some gemstones and practices to address grounding in the here and now. You can also regulate your energy by placing or holding Crown gemstones, like Serpentine, Smoky Quartz, Lodolite, or Dark Agate, near your head to focus the energy and funnel it down into your body. You can even place a stone right on the top of your head and balance it there like the old-fashioned posture exercise of balancing and walking with a book on your head. In fact, it can be a good test of how balanced your body is: if the stone falls off your head, you might need to focus on the lower chakras first.

You can accompany or treat your stones with the scents of Cedarwood or Patchouli to help draw them to ground. As you hold your stones close to your Crown Chakra, imagine that they are lightning rods channeling the electrical energies of the atmosphere from the sky into your body and discharging them back into the air. Picture the crown spinning like a wheel around your spinal axle levelly about three feet around you in all directions, with the stone at the center of the axle holding the spin at a steady speed. Breathe your intention to balance your Crown Chakra into the stone, and, if you are inclined, wear it close to remind you of that intention. Perhaps a headband or earrings with your chosen gemstone would be a good choice, as they will be close to your Crown.

Under-Energized Crown

An under-energized Crown Chakra may cause you to feel isolated, lonely, and disconnected. You might feel as if no one understands you or that you are surrounded by a cloud of confusion. You might also feel stuck and that you are lacking guidance. Just as with an over-energized Crown, you might even suffer physical symptoms, like migraines or sinus headaches and disruptions to your sleep cycle. Often, an under-energized Crown manifests as too much sleep and a lack of physical energy in general. You may have a hard time meditating if you can even bring yourself to try, as you also may experience barriers to trying—like mental blocks or a lack of motivation.

When your Crown is under-energized, you can feel distrust for your intuition and inner voice or for any messages you might interpret as coming from outside yourself (such as from the divine, the Universe, or your spiritual self). If you believe strongly in a higher power, you might feel completely disconnected from these energies and feel an overwhelming fear of death. Often, under-energized Crowns can manifest as a feeling of panic and stress, even when your energy might be at an all-time low.

To balance an under-energized Crown Chakra, focus on building an authentic rapport with what lies beyond the physical world. Meditation, prayer, journaling, or even talking to your *Self* as if you are talking to a close friend can serve as excellent tools. The trick is to find something that feels authentic to you. If prayer reminds you of a strict religious upbringing that scarred you in some way, then prayer might not be the best place for you to start (though you might begin to infuse stones to help you "reprogram" how you think about and use prayer). Because meditation can be so difficult for folks with an underactive Crown, guided meditations might be helpful—particularly ones that take you on a narrative journey to meet a guide or a version of your Higher Self.

If you feel more comfortable communicating with your Subconscious Mind, try journaling or asking yourself questions. One great trick is to write a question you have for yourself with your *dominant writing hand*, and then use your *nondominant writing hand* to answer it on the same page. Another approach to connecting with your Subconscious Mind is to assign it a task: say to yourself, "Subconscious, I am assigning you the task of figuring out what the best approach to [X] problem would be." Then direct your Conscious Mind to something gentle and mundane, like sorting your stones and crystals, mindfully doing the dishes, or counting the types of trees you find on a nature walk. This gives your Subconscious the chance to work without being led by the Conscious.

Employ sensory tools like singing bowls or stargazing to activate and amplify your Crown Chakra energy. If you are open to it, you might even try divination using oracle or tarot cards or a regular playing card deck. Ask questions and use the cards' symbolic imagery to speak to your Subconscious.

You may find it helpful to scry with your stones. Draw a circle on a piece of paper and gently cast some of your smaller crystals into the circle. The closer to the center a stone is, the more aligned it is with you, so you might look at what stones land where and what each stone means to you personally, to get a sense of "where you're at." You can do the same exercise by making a simple drawing of your body outline and casting stones into that to intuit where you might be balanced or out of control. In both of these examples, the circle and the body outline and the stones you cast into it are simply a way to communicate with your subconscious—it gives your cognitive mind something to think about while your gut or your intuitive mind essentially decides what something might mean to you and how you might work for your greater good. Just remember to set that intention first! Specific stones for energizing your underactive Crown include Selenite, Amethyst, Clear Quartz, Kunzite, Golden Rutile Quartz, and Clear Topaz. Try combining these with herbs like Lavender or essential oils such as Frankincense and Myrrh to connect with your purple energy center.

THIRD EYE STATES

The Third Eye Chakra exists in the space at the center of your forehead between your eyes and radiates typically from the top of the head down to about the chin. It is associated with intuition, astral senses, and the innate mind. It is typically represented by a dark blue or indigo color, so stones like Iolite, Lapis Lazuli, and Indigo Gabbro are excellent stones for this area.

Balanced Third Eye

A balanced Third Eye is quite powerful, as it indicates that you are manifesting your dreams, holding strong mental and cognitive energies, envisioning your success, and achieving goals. When your Third Eye is in balance, you are in a position to tap into your subtle or astral senses. You may see your desired future and manifest that future into reality. Imagine now that the energy of your Soul comes into your body through your Heart. The mission of your life's purpose can be visualized in the Third Eye, and you can then use that visualization to manifest the divine into form. The Third Eye is the space where cosmic energy forms into mental visions, physical sensations, or astral or subtle sensations. It is through the Third Eye that you will find the seeds of tangible creation. When your Third Eye is balanced, you are quite clear about your goals as you can "see" them and you are filling your mental movie screen with images and memories that support your highest good. Essentially, a balanced Third Eye is one which is helping you to stay in the vibration of health, love, harmony, achievement, and wellness by virtue of what it allows to be "seen" in this space.

Core Issue for Third Eye Imbalance

As the Third Eye is your energy center of intuition, clairvoyance, and inspiration, an imbalanced Third Eye means you may feel either disconnected from intuition or completely overwhelmed by it. You may develop a sort of tunnel vision which limits the paths of fulfillment in your life. This can easily happen when you focus your energy on manifesting something too limited, such as the love of a specific person as opposed to an abundance of love in general or curing a specific illness instead of feeling the benefits of good health and wellness. On the other hand, in an under-energized state, you might experience an inability to see yourself in a fulfilling job or relationship.

While you are working on an imbalanced Third Eye, it can help to program your stones and crystals with the intention to witness the subtle language of the Universe and empower your role as a creator. If your Third Eye is imbalanced, you may have difficulty just trusting people or yourself, so start by tuning into yourself. Use stones to help you *listen* to your inner voice and the communication of your Heart Chakra as it expresses to you your sincerest goals. Sometimes we *want* things with our emotions or analytical mind that don't actually serve our best selves or healthy lives. An imbalanced Third Eye may cause us to miss the cues that we may be desirous of things that aren't in our best interests—a few infused stones can serve as physical reminders of our intention to hear what our Soul is truly asking to experience.

Over-Energized Third Eye

You've heard the phrase "seeing is believing"? Well, an over-energized Third Eye Chakra is linked to seeing mental images that are so rich and vivid in detail that you believe wholly in them even if you know these ideas will not serve your highest good. You might begin picturing worst-case scenarios as the default, focusing on all the possible challenges you might face while working toward a goal. You might be replaying all the times you imagine yourself to have failed or been hurt in some way and find you are reliving past traumas which hold you in a space of disempowerment. This disempowered self-view extends to the circumstances around you as well as how you might even view yourself. You can see the danger here if you hold yourself in your mind's eye to be sick, unhealthy, unlucky, unloved, unsupported, impoverished, or limited. You aren't even likely to realize when something good comes along—your perspective will be so focused on the negative that you might not even catch a glimpse of the success. And as this area is tied to intuition and expansive thinking, an over-energized Third Eye may lean toward "seeing" and believing" too much in everyday signs without enough inner discernment. In other words, you might begin making patterns where there are none to see. For example, we can subconsciously train ourselves to view 11:11 on the clock each day and take it as a sign.

To balance an over-energized Third Eye Chakra, take a disciplined approach to "adding the good" to your mental movie screen and envisioning your success and abundance. You might start with Lapis Lazuli, which is an indigo stone flecked with gold, symbolic of the sacred inner voice of divinity that resides in each of us on Earth. To act with discipline, carry the stone in your pocket or wear it as earrings or in a headband to gently guide your focus back to positive thinking. Imagine pairing a stone with this intention—you might click two stones together or simply rub your thumb into the surface of the stone to create an interruption of the pessimistic mental movie you may be playing for yourself. Use the stones to remind yourself: "No, I will no longer entertain images and memories which do not support my goals. I now only allow images and visions which support my highest good."

If you are unable to make the jump from one end of the visualization spectrum to the other, then simply reject the negative mental image and fill the space instead with anything that makes you feel good. Imagine your stones are there to build a wall between you and a negative or pessimistic self-view. In other words, if you keep experiencing images of pain or failure but are unable to authentically create images of success, then start by telling yourself you reject the mental picture that is causing you harm. Then focus on another person who inspires you in some way or an image of peace and bliss. Clearly this is a useful skill for many tasks, such as planning a road trip or scoping a project with deadlines. Be sure to focus your energy and the intention you place on your stones toward the positive solution rather than on the struggle or the challenge you must overcome. Otherwise, you won't be focused on your goal and will be expending visualization energy toward failing.

One of the ways you balance an over-energized Third Eye is to anchor it to the energy of the Sacral Chakra and get the energy flowing through your heart and into your body. Gemstones such as

Peach Moonstone, Peach Aventurine, Morganite, or Pink or Grey
Banded Agates are excellent for soothing an over-energized Third
Eye. Essential oils or aromas that are grounding, such as Peppermint
or Citrus, are helpful for bringing clarity and waking up the senses to
the moment rather than projecting future scenarios. You might even
"dress" your stones in these essential oils or herbs to pair the crystal
energies with the vibration of the scent. Audio frequencies of Alpha
and/or Theta brain waves are also very helpful to utilize in calming
this energy point.

Under-Energized Third Eye

When the Third Eye is under-energized, you may feel generally
unable to visualize or manifest your next steps. You may feel
disempowered and like you are a victim of circumstance. It is as
though you cannot "see" the light at the end of the tunnel, and you
may even feel you need to follow a path others have set, even if it may
not be the best for you personally. You may have trouble believing in
yourself. Where an over-energized Third Eye has you believing you
can do anything (including the wrong thing) to achieve your outcome,
an under-energized Third Eye causes you to miss seeing things and
get lost in the proverbial darkness.

An under-energized Third Eye Chakra will also hinder your
inspiration. If you do have flashes of inspiration, you will often
dismiss them right away. For example, if you dream of becoming a
musician, you may see yourself recording a song but quickly move
that mental image to disbelief. You may tell yourself "It would be
impossible to support myself as an artist! It's too complicated to
promote and share my work." Or you may reflect on how your
parents couldn't afford music lessons for you when you were a child,
and that somehow this set you too far back to make progress (but
remember! The famous painter Grandma Moses didn't pick up a

paintbrush until she was seventy-eight years old! You can pick up a guitar right now. It *is possible, even if you tell yourself it is not)*. If you do keep the dream of becoming a musician while your Third Eye is in this condition, then you will likely only be able to think about ways that you have seen others accomplish this goal and block yourself to other potential solutions to your quest.

To balance an under-energized Third Eye, try journaling, which is an excellent tool to record a desire and continue to focus on it manifesting it daily—there are many excellent options of crystal pens you might use to write in your book. You might also use an Obsidian needle or blade to write your intention into the wax of a candle before you light it. Dedicate a page and a candle to a theme of your ideal self: how you want to be seen, how you want to handle challenges, or how you wish to develop your skills and gifts. Tell yourself, "I live in a state of comfort and peace. I easily handle all challenges and turn every potential 'loss' into a 'lesson.' I am divinely connected to the messages of the universe and follow my heart to achieve my desires. I see myself achieving. I see how easy it was. I see my Soul's fulfillment."

As you work with stones, focus on the successes you've watched others achieve—just be careful not to attach your stones to a singular narrative of success. There is a very successful public figure who shared that, when she was working to manifest her own success, she would focus on another woman whom she admired and who achieved success in a similar field. It is important to let the intention for your personal success unfold in the most ideal way for you and not the prescription of this other narrative. You cannot follow the direct path of others, but they can offer ideas.

Lapis Lazuli, Amethyst, Iolite, Indigo Aura Quartz, Blue Tiger's Eye, and Indigo Gabbro are strong stones for Third Eye energy. Essential oils and herbs such as Bay, Sage, Frankincense, and Juniper are also known for working to activate this area. Audio frequencies such as those for Gamma brain waves are known for enhancing visualization, and the note A is known to work with the Third Eye.

THROAT CHAKRA STATES

The Throat Chakra is aptly located just below the chin and above the collar bone. Some traditions combine the Throat and Third Eye Chakras, with both represented by a blue hue. We envision the Throat Chakra as the center for communication, logic, and "learned knowledge," governed by a light blue color. Stones such as Celestite, Aquamarine, Dumortierite, Blue Fluorite, and Blue Calcite can harness the balanced energies of the Throat Chakra. Try wearing one of these stones set in a choker or strung from a short pendant or strand of beads.

Balanced Throat

If your Throat Chakra is balanced, you are able to express yourself and think in ways that support your highest good, as well as interpret communication from others in ways that align you to your best. You don't tend to take things too personally, and you seem to have a sense for what people mean by the words they use. You don't find yourself insulted by the little things, and you are able to speak, act, and express your truth. A balanced Throat Chakra doesn't just govern the words we choose to say or what we hear; it also represents other forms of expression, like dialogue, art, writing, clothing, and body language. If the Universe sends a Soul message to us from our Heart and it begins to take conscious shape in our Third Eye, then the Throat is where we begin to express that shape into being by speaking or sharing it with others.

This chakra is also representative of your self-talk. In an over-energized state, you limit your own potential through your thoughts and how you talk to yourself. Even in jest, it is not beneficial to call yourself stupid, broken, anxious, nervous, or poor, because the language you use to express these things is all energetic. Expression is part of the process of creation, so it's wise to only express what you truly want. Stay solution-focused and positive with your self-talk. Stones are a great tool in this work because they can serve as physical reminders of words you speak over them.

Core Issue for Throat Imbalance

When your Throat is imbalanced, you don't feel you can speak or understand the truth. You may feel confused or misunderstood in general. It may seem like a paradox: you need to know what you want and focus your attention on that desire, but you also need to hold space for things to unfold without holding too tight a grip on how you want them to play out. Give things room to manifest as they will, because it's not just your own energies at work in the world, but the energies of everyone around you, too. Essentially, know what you want and think and speak in ways that support you, but be open to going with the flow and the inevitable unexpected detour and don't stress over every little detail.

An imbalanced Throat Chakra means you may say things you don't mean. It may mean you are trying to please others, and you may feel frustrated with people. If you truly want to be a musician, you must talk about music, listen to it, read about it, and learn how to read in musical language, and you also need to allow music to be expressed within yourself at the same time. The mind has a habit of "running away." Speaking the truth and listening for it are the critical components of a properly balanced Throat.

Over-Energized Throat

Ever find yourself talking to someone who seems to want to tell you all about her favorite television show, the kidney surgery her cat needs, as well as every detail of the kitty's daily medical issues and her political position on fracking before you can even ask how she's doing? Chances are the person you are imagining right now is dealing with an over-energized Throat Chakra. When the Throat is over-energized, it may overwhelm us with *content.*

An over-energized Throat Chakra may also manifest as neurotic behavior and overly analytical thinking, or more accurately, as *overly analytical speaking,* since the thoughts are typically disconnected in this state. You might feel hyperfocused on trying to understand the *meaning* of things. It is as though you are trying to understand too much and draining your energy constantly thinking of scenarios: *When will this happen? When will I meet the One? When will my partner ask me to marry them? Will it be this month? How will they ask me? Where will it be? Will I get this job? Will I move?*

Constantly thinking, or again, *talking about* when something will happen is not only draining but also counterproductive to your energy work. This not only disempowers you, it sacrifices your focus. You are essentially hoping something will happen *to* you rather than taking steps to bring it into your life directly. For example, if you have a goal of becoming a parent, you might be ignoring red flags from your potential co-parent and putting too much pressure on the situation. When your Throat is over-energized, you are putting a lot of heat or energy into your goal but not necessarily bringing that goal to a productive boil.

Likewise, an over-energized Throat Chakra may be trying to command another person to its will. That is, you might be talking in order to convince and coerce others to change course to what *you* want. *You cannot change people.* You may be expressing things abrasively, coming off as harsh, overly assertive, or "negative" to those around you. You may complain of trying very hard to communicate a need or interest but feeling wholly misunderstood by others or stuck in uncomfortable patterns.

To sooth an over-energized Throat Chakra, bring awareness to your current patterns of self-talk. Neuro-Linguistic Programming, sometimes shortened to NLP, works with the way your brain interprets language and the power that language has to manifest change. If we tell you right now to *not* think about a slice of steaming-hot apple pie with a dollop of vanilla ice cream slowly melting in its middle, we bet we can tell you exactly what you are imagining right now. It's not because you're a pessimist or a rebel. It's because you visualized the suggested idea as you read the words above, and, before you could tell your brain to reject it, you had to first manifest the idea in your mind. Effective NLP is particularly effective when your Throat Chakra is over-energized because you can flip that hyperactive energy to a positive outcome if you change your language.

Acquire a flat-backed sliver of Aquamarine or Blue Topaz and affix it to the cover of your favorite journal. By journaling, you can open a dialogue with your unseen potential. Try using your dominant hand to write a question you have for yourself, then use your nondominant hand to write the answer. Using your nondominant hand in this way may trigger your Throat Chakra to release the truth and balance itself. Write in the positive and affirmative, even if you are reflecting on something in your past: "I chose to manifest happiness, a loving relationship, and a career path which supports my highest good, and I am open to all the benevolent paths by which these goals will reach me. I understand that there are things working behind the scenes, in my favor and for my highest good, and I trust these to unfold in divine timing and coordination."

Gemstones that can calm this energy include: Peach or Rainbow Moonstone, Peach Aventurine, Pink or Grey Banded Agate, Morganite, Chrysocolla, or Pale Blue Chalcedony. Essential oils and herbs such as Chamomile or Lavender have calming frequencies like those of Alpha and/or Theta brain waves. Try wire-wrapping a piece of Blue Chalcedony to the top of your pen while you journal.

Under-Energized Throat

Conversely, an under-energized Throat disrupts your ability to express yourself from a place of authentic vibration. This includes communication like speaking and texting, as well as all the nonverbal ways we express ourselves, including your personal style or artistic abilities. If you have an under-energized Throat, you may be having trouble speaking candidly due to discomfort, fear, or anxiety. You may have difficulty forming thoughts or trying to get a word into a conversation. Or you may have writer's block and find it difficult to write more than a few words in an email or text. You may want to express something you can't get out, such as when you need to say something you know will be painful for someone to hear. An under-energized Throat can cause anxiety, avoidance, and a general excess of quietude.

It could be that you might be essentially mimicking the thoughts or expressions of a family member or friend, or perhaps a celebrity you wish you could emulate. You might also find yourself going along with the mob mentality rather than shaking things up with your unique view because you feel it is too different or doesn't belong. Accepting what others say as truth and taking on their beliefs happens in this state, and you may find yourself easily swayed by media sources toward false fear of scarcity when there is no true need for fear. You may find you are gullible or easily manipulated.

To achieve balance, start by projecting your mental plan and focus on your Subconscious Mind through meditation and listening exercises. Talk to yourself: Assign your Subconscious Mind the task of rejecting any imposed belief that is not truth. Visualize a golden halo around your head to protect yourself from thoughts imposed from without that do not support the greatest good of the Self. Infuse a stone with the intention of keeping you safe from unintended words, whether they are those you might speak or those you might get from someone else. Give your intention to the stone, and trust that it will guide you, because the stone is a reflection of you. You can trust *yourself.*

Gemstones such as Blue Calcite, Blue Fluorite, Celestite, or Apatite can increase the power of this work. Essential oils or teas such as Peppermint or Ginger are also helpful. The note of G is stimulating for this chakra, and binaural beats which utilize 741 Hertz activate this region and can raise it to a higher vibration.

HEART CHAKRA STATES

The Heart Chakra is sometimes referred to as the Heart center because it exists at essentially the center of our body. Imagine yourself seated in the lotus position with your legs folded at the knees on either side of your hips. In this position, your limbs are folded toward your torso and your torso creates the chakra body that allows Shakti, or life essence, to flow up and down and out from yourself. Stones associated with the Heart Chakra are all green stones, including Chrysocolla, Chrysoprase, Emerald, Jade, and Aventurine. Some practices, though, lean to using pink in this region, and it is thus not uncommon to also find Rose Quartz connected to Heart Chakra work as well.

Balanced Heart

When your Heart Chakra is balanced, you have a clear sense of
what you desire and are aligned with self-discovery. At the core, a
balanced Heart feels joyful and hopeful. You feel you are on the path
to achieving your Soul's innermost goals, and a sense of fulfillment
swells within you. You feel love and compassion for others, but you
understand the need to put yourself and your needs first in order to
maintain your overall well-being. To help others, you must first be well
enough in yourself to have the energy to help, and a balanced Heart
helps you realize that. By being true to yourself, you allow others to
do the same.

At the same time, a balanced Heart Chakra does not mean that the
world has become a Technicolor Pollyanna story free of heartache
and pain. These emotions are unfortunately a part of reality, but
when your Heart is balanced, you are best prepared to cope with
them well. You will approach situations without judgment and with
faith that you are doing your very best and that those around you
are as well. A truly awakening Heart will see all "good" and "bad"
experiences as opportunities for growth and deeper understanding.
When the Heart is aligned, you know there is no such thing as
failure: There are only opportunities to change, evolve, learn, grow,
and emerge.

Remember, the Heart Chakra is one of two points in your energy
system directly linked to the Soul, and when it is balanced, you
will find it much easier to communicate with your truest intentions
and desires. While it is healthy to be *discerning*, you won't judge
your messages as good or bad and will see them with intention and
decisiveness. The world won't be happening *to you* because you
will be an active agent in your own evolution. A balanced Heart
communicates the soul's desires in sometimes unexpected ways, or
the message itself may be slightly confusing to our cognitive brains.

You might feel compelled to reach out to an old friend, take a trip, or simply go left at an intersection where you usually would take a right. In balance, we simply receive these messages from within so as to manifest something along our paths that the Heart knows will guide us in the right direction. When the Heart is balanced, you have faith.

Core Issue for Heart Imbalance

Core issues related to imbalance can be impacted by difficulty in either direction of the chakra axle. If the Root is imbalanced and the body is having difficulty grounding or feels airy and weightless, then the imbalanced Heart may amplify all the issues in the chakras above it, from distrust to a disconnection from a sense of value. If the Crown is imbalanced and the spirit and body are too heavy or dragged down by routine and obligation, then the imbalanced Heart may amplify the issues of the chakras below it. This can manifest as an overreliance on the physical senses, a sense of hedonism, or a lack of interest in creating.

The Heart Chakra itself is summarized by the concept of (and connection to) Divine love and soul purpose. An imbalanced Heart means messages of love, self-love, and personal desire are being disrupted. We must love ourselves enough to understand we "deserve" love and that nothing we have done or will do robs us of that worthiness, but an imbalanced Heart can be confused about that core sense of value. We must also build a relationship with the Heart and listen to the requests it makes. Both the under-energized and over-energized Heart Chakra has the risk of pushing away people who love us or who only want to see us succeed.

Over-Energized Heart

An over-energized Heart can sometimes cause us to miss warning signs that something or someone is not for the best. It can feel like we are giving more than we are receiving or that we are "pouring from an empty cup," which can be connected to self-sacrifice in the extreme. A common theme you may experience might be "living for" someone else in some way, such as your child, a lover, or a parent. You might feel you are working in a job that you dislike. Let's say your family always pressured you to be a doctor, but, in your soul, you really wanted to be a singer in Vegas. A sign of an over-energized Heart might be sacrificing that stage performance to do those clinical rotations instead of the goal within your own heart. It's true you probably don't love your job every second of every day, but being tied to one that is not fulfilling can possibly burn out the Heart. Eventually, you will face a reckoning.

Another common symptom of an over-energized Heart is criticism. The Heart center is discerning and makes choices, but when that choice is on overdrive, discernment gives way to cynicism. You judge yourself so harshly that it is projected onto others, so if you are unhappy with your body, you might find you are pointing out what you consider to be the flaws in someone else's body. Parents in particular can over-energize and therefore burn out the Heart by giving excessively to their children, and it can be easy to fall into the trap of projecting onto those we love what we expect of ourselves. You cannot see a truth in anyone if it does not exist within you first.

To harmonize an over-energized Heart, release your judgments, unrealistic expectations or self-standards, and attachments to particular outcomes or situations. Many times, the concept of nonattachment can be confusing; it may sound like someone is suggesting that you stop caring, but that's not the case at all. Nonattachment is unconditional love. The way a mother loves a child is unconditional, yet there are still boundaries. If a child were to test the parent by hitting, the parent would not stop loving the child, but they would shift the situation to eliminate the harm. A powerful phrase you can carry to manage your Heart center is this: "I love you, but I will not let you hurt me." Whether you declare this out loud to someone pushing your personal boundaries or internally as a method of preserving your own energy, you are discerning. You are separating love from self-sacrifice. If you can see this perspective and resonate with the ability to love without attachment, then you can also understand the other side of the situation and fulfill your Heart-based path.

Pink stones which work well to balance the hyperactive Heart include Rose Quartz, Pink Agate, Mangano Calcite, and Rhodonite. Likewise, the chakra's green energetic resonance draws to it stones like Chrysoprase and soft Green Opal, too. Calming essential oils and teas such as those with Lavender, Rose, or Jasmine are excellent for soothing the overactive Heart Chakra. Meditations which connect you to your soul purpose or desire, or those which guide you to hear the messages of divine self-love, also help with an over-energized Heart.

Under-Energized Heart

An under-energized Heart can leave you completely isolated. It can be similar to building a wall around you, which may start out as protection from heartache and evolve over time into self-imposed isolation and loneliness. You are especially at risk when you experience a major life loss, such as suffering heartache, grief, guilt, rejection, or trauma, all of which can lead to difficulty in fully loving yourself. When under-energized, the Heart is somewhat numb and disconnected from the limitless universal energy of love. That is not to imply that you are unable to love or feel loved, but what energy you may be experiencing has a barrier. In some cases, this means you might be rejecting abundance, health, or healthy relationships because you feel unworthy. If an over-energized Heart is receiving the requests of the Soul but still denies them, the under-energized Heart does not even realize there are messages coming in the first place.

While love in this context can include romantic or chemical love and lust, this chakra's function is primarily concerned with nonjudgmental appreciation for all the unique facets of each soul. You may be blocked from feeling complete acceptance and unconditional love. You might not be resonating with others, or you may no longer see clearly the value your unique self brings to the entire world. Perhaps you have lost a loved one and blame yourself in some way, or you have been hurt in past relationships and are caught up in rejection with a mindset of blame. You might be hard on yourself and may be disconnected from your inner child. An under-energized Heart Chakra can make you forget that you are in charge of taking care of yourself just as if you had been handed the responsibility of caring for a baby. How should you treat yourself?

Meditate on your inner child and send love back to yourself. If you have any stones in your life that you've carried for a long time, or, perhaps if you live in a place near where you grew up where you could pick a stone up, it can be helpful to use that stone as a communication tool with your younger self. Since stones are so timeless—they have existed long before us and will be here long after we are gone—you might imagine that it is like a time machine. Talk to it and give it the love you need in the past or the future; ask it to communicate that love to your younger or older self. Treat it like a messenger and breathe your message into it with a whisper. Guided meditations or working with a healer are usually very helpful for this practice of communing with younger versions of ourselves. Gemstones such as Green Calcite, Green Tourmaline, Turquoise, Rhodochrosite, and Emerald are excellent in working with this state of energy, as are essential oils and herbs which combine the frequency of love with a kick; something like Rose and Cinnamon, or Jasmine and Ginger.

SOLAR PLEXUS STATES

The Solar Plexus Chakra exists just under the rib cage and above the navel and relates primarily to our sense of confidence and independence. It also is the center of your artistic and creative self. Following the energetic rainbow, this region is depicted by a sunshine yellow color and thus includes stones like Sunstone, Citrine, and some varieties of Calcite.

Balanced Solar Plexus

A balanced Solar Plexus indicates not only healthy confidence, personal power, and independence, but also an authentic resonance with being the person you truly want to be. If you have the goal of becoming an artist, with a balanced Solar Plexus, you truly *are* an artist. You already see yourself this way. You use the word "artist" to define yourself when people ask you, and you move and act in ways that support the vibration of your daily creative energy flow. Because the Solar Plexus is tied to the Self, a balanced chakra means a sense of balanced identity. You are "you," complete with your life experiences and soul purpose, the unique elements of your upbringing, the challenges you've faced as well as your successes, and everything else that makes up your original blend. With a balanced Solar Plexus, your energy is actively embodying the person you were meant to be.

Core Issue for Solar Plexus Imbalance

Because the Solar Plexus relates to the self and the sense of harmoniously and independently working with others, an imbalanced Solar Plexus tends to mean disharmonious interactions and a lack of self-worth. Just as an over-energized Solar Plexus might make a person feel an extreme need for independence, an under-energized chakra will make you feel dependent on someone or something else. Focus on the balance between taking action and responsibility for yourself and the fact that some goals require assistance, such as from teachers or mentors who can provide us with quality feedback.

Over-Energized Solar Plexus

This may show up as a strong desire for independence. You feel like you can do everything entirely on your own, even if you likely could get much further with much less stress if you allowed yourself the support of other people. Excess energy that should be directed toward achieving your creative goals builds up and compels you to avoid others. The energy will churn and grind as you continue to try to remain in isolation. It may not even be purposeful; many times, the over-energized Solar Plexus tricks you into believing you are alone. Even the coffee you might drink in the morning was packaged by someone before it was sold in the store where you bought it, and, before that, it was grown by a farmer who got the land from someone else.

You may not even have a clear understanding of your goals, including how to achieve them or where to put your active energy to allow for their success. You might also find you are attaching too much to the process and not enough to the desired outcome. If you are rejecting support, you may just need to reach out for help. There is a level of "control freak" that seems to manifest when this chakra amps up. You will not appear to be obsessed with control, but you will brush off every piece of constructive criticism or advice you receive as if the person providing the feedback doesn't know what they are talking about. The reason you are rejecting this feedback is because you are temporarily stuck in a belief that everything must be done through your own actions, but your actions will not be enough to reach the desired goal.

Grinding is a key word for this energetic state. You will feel as though you are accomplishing a lot, but when you do a tally of your completed tasks at the end of the day, you'll likely find you haven't accomplished very much at all and certainly not as much as you thought you did. If you fill your day with to-do lists but you are not focused on the ultimate goals behind each of those to-do items, you are not going to create the space for the energy of your day to move in the direction of growth and support.

To balance an over-energized Solar Plexus, it is helpful to set an intention each morning, before you even get out of bed, that you will direct your actions to fulfill your soul's desires. Instead of focusing on all the tasks to complete in just one day, zoom out and focus on a goal for the week, month, or year. Each morning, recommit to that goal. This way you are not creating or recreating a goal every day, but rather focusing on the smaller tasks that stack up to achieve a longer-term goal.

Find a stone that resonates with you for long-term work. Hold this stone in your palms above your Solar Plexus and breathe slowly. Imagine you are breathing into the stone itself as you fill your abdomen with each inhalation. Exhale for just a little bit longer than it takes to inhale. This stone is going to remind you of the goal you set so that each time you see it, feel it in your pocket, or reach out to touch it, you are repeating the mental message of your overarching goal.

Now, craft an active, positive self-goal that you will repeat each morning while attuned to your stone. You should write this statement in the present tense, as though you already have achieved it. For example, you might say "I am a happy and successful business owner." Recite this daily and follow it up with a direct request to your stone. Ask your stone to help you in some way. Think of it as asking a favor of a dear friend, and repeat this process daily. Don't forget to thank your stone for its help each day.

Blue Kyanite, Lepidolite, or Grey Agates are excellent for calming this chakra point, as are points of pale Amethyst. If you are working with a terminated stone, hold the pointed end of the stone so that it is facing outward from the Solar Plexus. Now direct your personal energy toward your ultimate goal. Essential oils and herbs that are soothing such as Chamomile, Lavender, or Bergamot are helpful to work with as well. Sounds can also support with this process, and we recommend really any music to which you feel personally connected as this will help you communicate with your inner self and help settle your over-energized state.

Under-Energized Solar Plexus

This state can have you feeling like a fraud. Ever hear of the concept of "imposter syndrome"? This occurs when a person is successful at a skill but doesn't believe she is successful, such as a brilliant business leader who perhaps dropped out of high school and therefore believes that her failure to complete school must mean she is not a "real" business success. An under-energized Solar Plexus can cause you to feel like you are not good enough, and, in extreme cases, it can even cause you to feel like you aren't "real."

You may feel less than confident in your ability to create in your life and evolve into the highest version of yourself. You also likely have an unhealthy attachment to the past—whatever it is you think shaped you and your identity. You may believe that since those elements are no longer in your life, you can't possibly be successful. You may have a low sense of self and determination. You attach to the struggles you have faced as well as what you have witnessed others experience, and you allow these debilitating beliefs to manifest even though you can clearly see they are not "true."

Just as with the Throat Chakra, where you hear or speak the truth, here, the Solar Plexus begins to solidify that belief in truth. It's as though the imbalance that you have in your Throat has begun to solidify and take root. From an outside perspective, you may seem stuck and unable to make effective changes. Many superstitions arise from one action becoming falsely attached to an unrelated outcome: I walked under a ladder, and, four days later, I was hit by a car. The connection is entirely in the mind. Don't believe everything you tell yourself. While implementing knowledge of patterns of causality and making changes is essential, sometimes shifting out of your negative patterns starts with remembering that not everything you believe is truth.

To balance an under-energized Solar Plexus, remember that not all actions are outward; it is fine to begin making changes in more subtle ways on the inside. You might change the music you have in your car or on your playlist to subtly shift your perspective to a different energy. Maybe you've been sad and listening to discordant tunes; now might be the time to shift that to angry or high-energy tunes to move your inner rhythm.

You might choose to have different conversations or conversation partners, or just change the words you use to describe things to yourself and others. Taking this approach creates a foundation for authentic shifts in how we see ourselves, and this will in turn impact the "bigger" or more physical actions we take to reach a goal. If you are not exactly an athlete but you want to participate in some kind of marathon, you might first research, study, and practice for the event: What are some good stretches to start? How should you hold your knees and arms? Do other runners in this marathon have a blog, or is there a news article about them? By starting in the mind, you can set the stage to move to action. Stones can be very helpful for this—particularly with the running example, as you can carry a stone in your clothing or palm as you run to harness that energy and focus its intention.

Gemstones which activate the Solar Plexus are Orange Calcite, Pyrite, Golden Quartz, Bumblebee Jasper, or Yellow Serpentine. Hiddenite is an excellent gem for bridging the Heart with the Solar Plexus and acting in ways that support the Heart's desire. Because the Solar Plexus is the first body or Earthly chakra below the Heart Center, it is often necessary to cycle your Solar Plexus energy upward to get these two energy centers aligned. Stimulating essential oils and herbs such as Citrus, Ginger, Clove, or Cinnamon work very well to amplify this space.

SACRAL CHAKRA STATES

The Sacral Chakra resides in the seat of the abdomen just below your belly button. It is associated with creation, emotion, primal instinct, and the connections you form with others in your life. In some schools of thought, this chakra is viewed as the Void from which things are birthed into existence, regardless of your physical anatomy. Because the Sacral is in many cases represented as a vessel, it is also a space where trauma and pain may energetically collect.

This region is most often depicted in a rich orange color, so orange stones such as Carnelian, Orange Selenite, Sunstone, Shaman Stones, Shiva Lingam, Aragonite, Fire Opal, and Fire Agate are easily aligned to this chakra.

Balanced Sacral

With a balanced Sacral Chakra, you are deeply in touch with your creative energy, you are likely experiencing healthy relationships, and, most importantly, you have the emotional maturity needed to navigate your life path. Because the Sacral is known as the Creative and Emotional center, when it is in balance, you will find it easy to create new works of art and that your emotions are stable and moving in a positive direction. In a state of balance, creating is more than just what we think of as the traditional arts; it is creating everything from a job search to a family to a new plan. If you are balanced, you are emotionally steady and able to bring your creative pursuits to fruition easily. You read the emotional cues of others well, and you are tuned into your own emotional expressions as a kind of barometer for whether you're on the right track. You've heard the phrase "gut instinct"? Well, it's no coincidence that a balanced Sacral Chakra includes a strong connection to the gut instinct—that deeply held knowledge of what is and what is not real.

The Sacral Chakra is also connected to the Earthly energy centers, and, when all of our chakras are aligned and balanced, we are spinning in the direction of positive self-growth and creation. All the chakras are in some way connected to the energy of creation, but the Sacral Chakra in particular is where we begin to manifest creation into something tangible—something you can touch. Two ways you might think of your balanced Sacral Chakra are as rich soil in spring, ready to sprout new and nourishing vegetables, or as clay ready to be shaped into a vessel or figure.

Core Issue for Sacral Imbalance

In an imbalanced condition, you are apt to either be emotionally scattered or, alternatively, numb. You likely won't be very good at reading the emotions of others, including social cues or body language, and your sense of healthy relationships may be out of whack. In this state, you might have "the wrong idea" about people close to you—you may think they mean more or less than they really do to your life's purpose, or you may invest your time and energy into people who don't care about you. A healthy relationship is not a dependent relationship but is instead focused on coexistence. When your Sacral Chakra is imbalanced, one or more people in a relationship may be overly attached to the others and might even rely on them for an emotional boost or sense of security. As with all chakras below the Heart center, it is specifically useful to work with stones on your person or held in your hands to ground and center when the Sacral is imbalanced, so you may wish to choose crystals that are palm or pocket-sized.

Over-Energized Sacral

With an over-energized Sacral Chakra, you may feel what is often described by professionals as "manic" or experience extreme emotional highs and lows. You may feel tossed around by emotional waves and may struggle to feel that anything happening in your life is real. While we do not mean to imply feelings are not real (since they certainly are), it can be helpful to remember that they are not *fixed* and, perhaps more importantly, that they do not always tell you the truth. Love turns to hate. Trust becomes jealousy, joy swings to sadness, and hope shifts to dejection when this state is over-energized. Feelings are guides to let us know that something is or is not right; they are like a compass helping us to see if our choices are aligned with our desires or if we're running off track. But we may not interpret our emotions correctly, or, in an over-energized state, we might put too much stock into them and not enough into the other elements of our health and well-being, like sensation, movement, routine, or cognition. In an over-energized state, it is very difficult to discern the meaning of the emotions, so instead we react from this emotional space without bringing in logic or the ability to see things from other perspectives.

You may also believe that you "need" someone or something to make you feel whole or to save or rescue you in some way. You may believe you need a person in order to feel happy or complete. The challenge is that it is not realistic to rely on a person in this way. And it is only when you feel whole even when totally alone that you are truly "complete" and balanced. When you seek out a relationship from a feeling of "need," you are attracting others who are perhaps looking to fulfill some kind of dependency, or you might manifest a partner who you then push away with your stress or neediness.

To balance an over-energized Sacral Chakra, start by objectively reviewing your emotions rather than identifying with them. Imagine yourself as an objective observer outside of your body, like a therapist examining you, the client, recumbent on the couch. What is this feeling trying to get across to you? What is the message? Why are you feeling this way?

Our emotions need to be validated and acknowledged, so be sure to do that in your responses: "I am feeling mad! I do not like this feeling! I am mad because when I came out from the store, my car had been hit by another, and they are nowhere in sight and no note has been left. I am mad that there are people out there who are so careless." Once validated by your independent observation, you should hopefully begin to feel the emotions lighten and begin to move on. This is a good opportunity to do intuitive work with stones. Fill a bag with crystals to which you feel attracted, and then close your eyes and reach into the bag with the intention of drawing out one or two stones that will help you balance your over-energized Sacral Chakra. The stones you select may symbolize the energy which needs your focus in order to ground. What did you draw out? What colors are they? What do they mean to you? What do you think they are telling you about yourself?

Another action might be to deliberately select a stone to work with that you fill up with all the things you think are "missing" in yourself and that you believe you need another person to supply to make you feel happy. The stone becomes a third party to fulfill your allegedly missing ideals. Write them down and assign them to the stone. Focus on how you can bring those energies into yourself *from yourself* rather than from the external world. Meditate with the stone. Allow yourself to feel calm, relaxed, and settled. You may find that you can fill this so-called missing piece in yourself by taking *yourself* on a date, joining a club, or starting a new hobby. Find your inner passion and indulge it mindfully. By doing so, not only are you creating a frequency of wholeness and self-love, but you are also setting yourself up to attract another person who is equally passionate and driven to develop their self.

There are many stones that can serve you as this is an Earthly chakra, so go first with your instincts. Gemstones such as Blue Chalcedony, Lepidolite, Aqua Aura Quartz, Green Apatite, Howlite, Light Purple Amethyst, or Lavender Quartz are excellent to calm this chakra, as are soothing essential oils and herbs such as Mints, Patchouli, Sandalwood, and Chamomile.

UNDER-ENERGIZED SACRAL

An under-energized Sacral Chakra may cause you to feel numb. There is a frequency of indifference and disinterest when this chakra is underactive, and you are likely to have difficulty in forming connections with others. Your creative energy will be low, and you may even reject your gut instinct when it arises, if you are even able to even perceive these instincts.

While there is certainly something to be said for the fact that we are all truly having our own experiences, the value of connecting with those outside ourselves is irrefutable. Other people all act as mirrors showing us pieces of ourselves and inspiring us in some way, and we serve the same purpose for others. Even connecting to a character in a book or film is a means of gently creating a bridge for the self to feel comfortable with others. Disconnection may stem from trauma associated with past relationships—perhaps you had a narcissistic parent, an abusive friend or partner, or some other harmful relationship that you are afraid to experience again, so you close yourself off from the possibility of all connections. If you identify with this, then therapy might be helpful to assist you with working through these experiences and moving beyond them. Energy work is a mindful practice that can help you serve yourself, but it is no substitute for medical or mental health services.

CLAY PIGEON STONE EXERCISE

To balance, try doodling on paper, cooking a creative meal, redecorating a room, or giving yourself a makeover. One activity you might pursue is the Clay Pigeon Stone Exercise. Begin by selecting a stone that represents your goal or ideal, and then pack air-drying clay around it, building the clay up into a blobby shape with a flat bottom. Let the clay dry in the sun as you imagine the stone inside of it as the truth or core of yourself. As the clay dries, imagine yourself letting go of the obstacles that prevent you from achieving your goals. Then, when it's fully dry, either carefully take a hammer to the clay or drop it on a hard surface to shatter the obstacle and reveal the valuable object within it. Dust off your stone and place it in a sunny window as a reminder of how you freed yourself from a blockage.

Emotional comprehension is also essential to amplifying an under-energized Sacral Chakra. At some point, emotions will need to have their outlet or you might explode. You have to be okay with what you are feeling and not judge those feelings, so using crystals (like Clear Quartz) that help you deflect judgment or release your emotional energy can help you focus and validate. Validating feelings does not mean you are giving them more power, but rather that you are allowing them to flow. In much the same way, a Clear Quartz amplifies or energizes any of the relaxation work we might do. We can then move to make changes, either internally or externally, as guided by our understanding of the cause of the emotional reaction.

Many gemstones serve to shake us out of this under-energized chakra. Carnelian, Orange Calcite, Shiva Lingam stones, and Geodes, as well as egg-shaped gemstones, are particularly excellent for stimulating this chakra. Geodes in particular are symbolic of the same inner, Earthly value exemplified by the Clay Pigeon exercise. Cracking open a Geode is an activity unto itself, one that can help us re-amplify the sparkle inside. Essential oils and herbs that energize us, such as Citrus and essential spice oils like Clove, Cinnamon, and Cardamom are all excellent tools to bring up a sluggish Sacral Chakra. High-energy music and dancing are also great tools to shake things up and recenter yourself.

ROOT CHAKRA STATES

The Root Chakra resides at the base of the spine and forms a kind of tripod with the sitting bones. The full wheel of the Root energy spins around the pelvis and extends down into the legs like the roots of a tree into the ground. This zone is primarily concerned with our sense of security, physical vitality, abundance, and ability to manifest in the Earth realm. Here, we draw up energy from the Earth to nourish and anchor ourselves and to invoke a sense of safety. Traditionally, this chakra is symbolized by red ochre or rust color (like the blood that carries important nutrients through our bodies). Red and brown stones like Jasper, Ruby, Garnet, Axinite, and Bronzite are connected to this chakra and serve it well. As the base of the energy axle, the Root is the strongest of the Earthly energies and represents all the things that help us feel we are part of the planet that supports us.

Balanced Root

Harmony and security around physical health and safety are at the core of a balanced Root Chakra. When you are in this state, you feel connected to the Earth and can access every resource and material support you might need to manifest your goals and well-being. You are able to process fear and anger in healthy ways and deal with these feelings as they flow into you. In a state of harmony, the Root, which relates to primal needs such as food, water, shelter and overall safety, causes you to feel secure and whole. This energy wheel also connects to family patterns and lineage and therefore helps you to break free of difficult family behaviors or patterns.

When balanced, you feel rooted to the Earth. Routines come easily to you and serve your needs. You rise and eat healthily—neither too much nor too little—and you give back to the Earth as well. You may grow plants or take care of animals. When you're balanced, you may even wish to volunteer your time to serve a charity that is important to you. Your relationships with others are grounded, and you feel safe with people. Likewise, when your Root is balanced, you also have a sixth sense when a person is not safe to be part of your environment, and you know just what to do to ensure your overall sense of security is maintained.

Core Issues for Root Imbalance

Fear and fight-or-flight reactions may be churning up your anxieties. In an over-energized state, you see fight—everything is a conflict that must be addressed head-on. In an under-energized state, you see flight—nothing feels safe, and you feel the need to "run away" from your problems. An imbalanced Root Chakra may cause you to fear facing your problems with logic. Instead, you may be attached to your problems and have difficulty releasing your limitations or being objective. Commonly, when you are in a state of transition, even for the development of your highest good, you likely feel afraid because things are changing and you therefore need to adjust. This is seen in "success crisis" situations where everything may be going well, but perhaps there is too great a quantity of these good and successful things to manage. Even good stress is stress and can contribute to a Root imbalance.

It is important to have a balance of understanding that safety is created through the building of your own foundations, so that when you fall, you know how to get back up again. At the same time, you must keep in mind that anything can happen at any time, unexpectedly, and so, from that perspective, safety is a necessary illusion. You are always best served by being adaptable and having healthy practices in place to validate and express feelings of fear, as well as to connect to the Earth and appreciate the experience of your life. When the Root is not balanced, you struggle with the illusion of safety and your sense of appreciation. You need both to flourish.

Over-Energized Root

If you are experiencing flashes of rage or irrational anger over what seem like unrelated issues, or if others describe you as having a short fuse, you might have an over-energized Root Chakra. Very often in these situations, you may seem to have this under control in public while inside you are screaming and seething with wrath. You may feel this as discomfort, as though you have no safe way to express anger without hurting or scaring others. These feelings come up particularly when there is even the slightest possible potential disturbance to your sense of fear of scarcity, whether it is related to an emotional relationship or a physical resource like food or water.

For example, a contractor working for a client on a project might feel extreme anger when the client comes back with some modifications to the job specifications. Because at the core the contractor feels rejected and fears for her overall safety, the client's requests are taken as a complaint and trigger her to experience a fight response. Another example might be if a diabetic person at a restaurant orders a coffee with Stevia and then discovers it has been served with full sugar; he might fly into a rage at the waiter as though it was some purposeful act intended to send him into a sugar coma. This anger response disrupts our vibration when things could be easily corrected with a calm conversation with the client or simply sending the coffee back for a corrected order.

Combining meditation and movement are excellent ways to balance an over-energized Root. Those who enjoy running might visualize their anger and fear being released with every footfall on the treadmill or running path. Those who prefer dancing may picture shaking off the anger and stress with every sway of the hips.

A common theme here is that you can bring a mindful awareness to your excessive anger and energy and choose to release the bad vibes through action and meditation. The energy is only "negative" or uncomfortable because it is stuck. On an energetic level, there is no good and bad; there is only a spectrum of frequencies and vibrations. If you don't process your energy, it will feel uncomfortable, but once you release it in a healthy movement, it is processed by the Earth and transmuted to a more positive state of being.

One way to picture this spectrum is by imagining a thermometer. There are some temperatures that might be too hot for a human, yet under the oceans there are thriving volcanic ecosystems where other life flourishes. While not strictly a stone but a mineral, you might use a piece of Coral for this work. As you meditate, imagine yourself sending this rage energy that is too hot for your human self down to the core of the Earth where it can flourish and nourish the creatures deep within.

STONE CONTAINMENT BOX ACTIVITY

Another exercise to soothe an over-energized Root is to create a Stone Containment Box. Begin by selecting a few stones (ideally with a flat bottom) that you can attach to your containment box. You might use an old tea box for this activity. Paint the box with symbols of peace and abundance; for example, you could paint it red and cover it with tree roots. Affix stones to the outside of the box with glue or string. Then, write down the things that are causing you to feel rage—you may even attach them to other stones with string—and mindfully place each rage-item in the box. As you close the lid, tell yourself, "These stones are guardians of my anger. They are the gatekeepers of my rage." Now imagine that any expression of anger you may have must first be checked by the stones (calmed by the Earth) before it is allowed to be verbalized or otherwise acted out. Each week, go through your containment box and review what's there. Are you still full of rage? If not, remove it. Tear up the paper it's written on and discard it. You no longer need it. Repeat this activity as often as necessary to shore up your Root.

Because the Root is the literal and figurative Earth, any stone at all can serve this energy if the stone represents Earth itself in your practice. It can help, however, to focus on gemstones with a particularly Earthy symbolism, such as Tree Agate, Indigo Gabbro, Ocean Jasper, Garden Quartz, and Smoky Quartz to soothe this over-energized chakra state. Essential oils which ease stress and anger such as Lavender, Peppermint, Clary Sage, and Cedarwood are also excellent for this chakra point. Calming music with a routine rhythm, such as classical compositions by Chopin or Mozart, may also be useful in serving this chakra in its purpose to soothe and calm and revitalize your security.

Under-Energized Root

When your Root Chakra is under-energized, you may have trouble connecting to the Earth and believing that you have all your needs met, whether material or emotional. You may have difficulty trusting that you have enough food or water, or you may feel generally unsafe and afraid. It may even be that you see the world as unfair, traumatic, limited, and sickening. When your Root is under-energized, you are also particularly susceptible to illness and a weakened immune system, so you might even consider seeing a doctor or nutritionist to keep illness at bay.

You can also feel spacey and out of touch and may not be able to see or feel your foundation—as though you are in orbit and not grounded at all. You may spend much of your time in a daze or daydreaming and feel uncomfortable with what you perceive as limitations here on Earth, such as time or monetary needs. You may also have trouble keeping to a schedule, remembering to eat, and making or keeping commitments. Others may describe you as "flighty," and it is very important to ground and center now more than ever.

When this chakra is under-energized, you are not clearly connected with your material well-being. You might, for example, understand that you are a spiritual being or that your time on Earth is limited, but you don't see a reason to ground. Why ground when it feels so good to be in orbit and take flight? After all, isn't the Divine connected to Heaven? Why be on Earth when you can soar? What is clearly missing in this perspective, however, is that self-awareness combines the Earthly with the Ethereal. We are part of the Earth—we are even elemental at our core, and we ultimately return to the Earth when we pass away. That sounds heavy and full of responsibility, but it is not as overwhelming as it might appear. All we need to do to ground this energy is to come into alignment with what our soul desires to fulfill, big or small, whether we are saving the world or simply enjoying it.

To activate an under-energized Root Chakra, savor the enjoyment of the Earth with reverence and appreciation. Practice mindfulness. Put all of your attention into the soles of your feet or into the stone you are holding between your hands. Enjoy your water, the air you breathe, and the foods which sustain you. Give thanks for and appreciate every comfort and lesson that you experience. Know that your enjoyment of the experience of life is really what it is all about. Eat nutritious foods such as root vegetables, carrots, beans, and fruits with appreciation for their aromas and textures as well as how they fuel your body. And remember the importance of taking in minerals as part of your nutrition plan, which is tantamount to ingesting gemstones for healing. Work with a professional nutritionist to ensure you have the right balance of Earthly minerals and nutrients in your diet to support the success of your unique body.

Guided meditations, particularly those with binaural support, that take you on journeys into the Earth or caves are excellent ways to ground and connect with your Root. Drumming, dancing, or meditating with gemstones such as Hematite, Axinite, Bronzite, Jasper, and River Quartz are excellent. Essential oils and herbs such as Angelica Root, Cedarwood, Pine, or other wood scents work very well to connect with the Root Chakra as well. A balanced Root is the foundation of well-being, so feel the Earth beneath your feet—

the Earth, which is made up of stones and organic material—and connect with the giant rock that sustains us all.

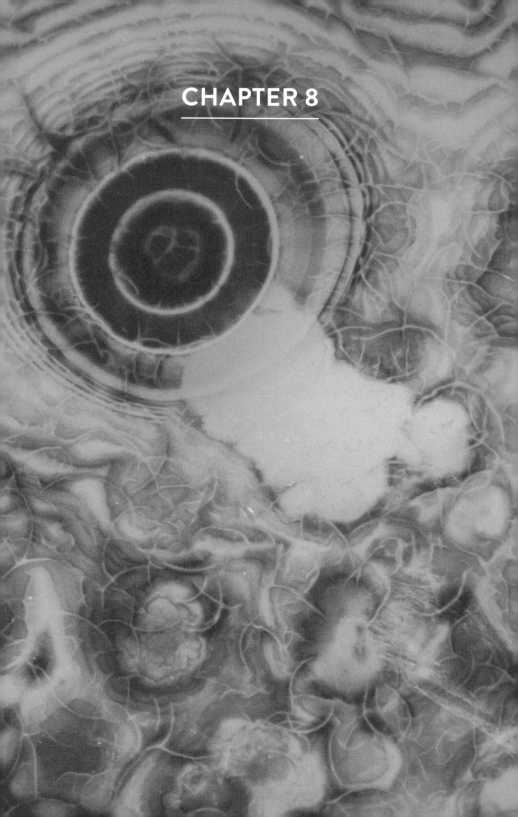

CHAPTER 8

MERIDIANS AND ENERGY POINTS IN THE BODY

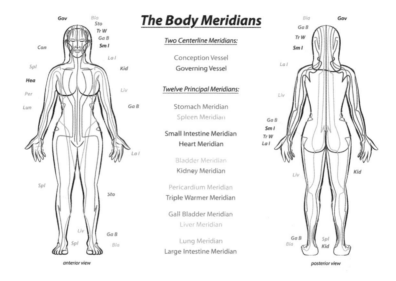

The Body Meridians

Two Centerline Meridians:

Conception Vessel
Governing Vessel

Twelve Principal Meridians:

Stomach Meridian
Spleen Meridian

Small Intestine Meridian
Heart Meridian

Bladder Meridian
Kidney Meridian

Pericardium Meridian
Triple Warmer Meridian

Gall Bladder Meridian
Liver Meridian

Lung Meridian
Large Intestine Meridian

anterior view   posterior view

Crystals can help us unlock trapped energy which might manifest as pain or knots by helping harmonize our emotional, habitual, and metaphysical relationship to different passageways within our bodies called meridians. These meridians and major joint areas are common concepts employed in the wellness and healing practices of acupuncture, Chinese medicine, chiropractic and myofascial care, and Reiki. To achieve a sense of well-being with any practice, including crystals, it is crucial to connect the dots of that experience to the body because our bodies are a great indicator of our inner selves. In accordance with the principle articulated by, "As above, so below," pain in the body is often coupled with emotional or spiritual pain and vice versa. As you bring awareness of your body into your crystal healing work, these pathways can help you identify where best to focus your actions and energies for maximum wellness and healing.

According to some interpretations of Chinese medicine,[12] which dates back thousands of years, meridians are the channels in the body through which life force flows in a way similar to how blood flows through our veins and arteries. There are two primary channels running from the center of the crown down to the bottom of the torso, with twelve meridians or branches related to specific organs. The joint points—which we will define as the ankles, knees, hips, elbows, shoulders, and neck—are areas where energy can become blocked and may be experienced physically as inflammation. There are also at least three meridians running along our appendages which pass through joints. Because the joints can bend or compress and can experience injury or stiffness, the flow of energy through these points can get jammed up just like traffic at an intersection. Just as a city planner or traffic controller might place signs and lights to get our vehicles safely from one point to another, so too a good energy healer can use crystals to pinpoint busy energy intersections and redirect movement. Polarity Therapy is one method of directing this energy. This can be an advanced practice, but even a novice can learn to use simple techniques to maintain harmony within the meridians and "go with the flow" of the body's system.

CRYSTAL ENERGY STREAM ACTIVITY

To get started thinking about the body's energy passageways, let's do a simple crystal visualization exercise. First, begin by determining your receptive and dominant hands. Your dominant hand is the one

---

12 *Huangdi Neijing*, or "The Yellow Emperor's Esoteric Scripture," written about two thousand years ago in a dated Chinese dialect that is not easily translated to Modern English, is the first known text to describe the preventative medicinal approach of Traditional Chinese Medicine. It is important to note that there are different schools of thought about meridians and energetic channels in the body, and the subject of Chinese Medicine is an advanced discipline requiring many years of study to master and thus cannot be adequately covered by us here.

you are most comfortable drawing or writing with, and your receptive hand is the other. If you are ambidextrous, then you may consider your right hand to be the dominant hand. If necessary, you may dowse with a simple crystal pendulum to determine what feels right to you. In esoteric teachings, the left mind and right side of the body are associated with the masculine energy of an individual, and the right mind and left side of the body are associated with a person's feminine energy. If that understanding resonates and you would like to continue working with the flow of energy from this concept, it is only important that you declare this is your choice. Think of it as speaking to your subconscious: Simply say aloud, "I choose my [x] side to be my dominant side."

Now, visualize a stream of energy moving through your body, coming into it from the receptive foot and hand and flowing out through the dominant ones. Once you have a good mental image of that energy pattern, place a Quartz Crystal in your nondominant hand and a piece of Jet or Obsidian in your dominant hand. Set the intention to cleanse your overall life force. Now imagine that each breath you draw in comes through the Quartz, amplified by it as the air passes into your body—really *breathe* into it—and imagine that same breath travels up one side and down the other, passing out of you through the Jet or Obsidian you are holding. If you are already practiced at drawing energy into yourself through crystal reception, you might add a step here which specifies something you wish to attract, such as love, abundance, a romantic partner, or a desirable outcome to a problem or situation. Simply picture this attraction coming in through the Quartz Crystal with each new inhale, and, when you exhale, picture your gratitude flowing back out through the Jet or Obsidian. You have now polarized your body's energy flow using crystals as the channels.

MUSCLE TEST STONE EXERCISE

Other ways to find blocks in the body include using a pendulum
or performing a muscle test. A muscle test uses your own body as a
dowsing rod. Place a simple stone in the palm of your dominant hand
(perhaps a Quartz Crystal, or even a street or beach stone you found
while out for a stroll). Now, bend your arm 90 degrees and flex your
bicep lightly. Using your other hand, press downward against your
wrist with what feels to you like equal pressure—so you are flexing
upward with your dominant hand and pressing downward against
it with your receptive hand. Now, tell yourself, "If my answer is yes,
move downward. If my answer is no, move upward" (or vice versa
as it suits you). When you are ready to ask yourself a question, you
can use this form of muscle testing or palm-dowsing to ask yourself
simple yes or no questions. For example, you might ask, "Am I happy
in this career?" "Do I really want this job?" "Is this the right crystal to
heal my broken heart?" "Do I feel this hand is my dominant hand?"
Muscle testing is another way to connect with your body for wellness
and to tune into what your body is trying to communicate to you. If
you're not yet sure which crystals resonate with you, don't worry. You
can start by placing a single crystal in your dominant hand and asking
if it's the "right" one for you. Keep doing this until you get a positive
response. Listen to yourself. You already know what's best. You just
need to clear the way to hear your own voice tell you the answers.

While we encourage you to study any topic you wish, you do not need
to comprehend every detail of the meridians to have a beneficial
effect on your energy. If you are interested in working with meridians
from their historical origins, it will be helpful to know that the Chinese
refer to our life energy as Qi, a variation we hear echoed in the
Egyptian concept of Ka (the soul) and the Japanese word Chi. Unlike
Westernized chakra work, which may have adapted over time into the

Four Humors once thought to rule over the body, which corresponded to the four elements of nature (Earth, Air, Fire, and Water), the Chinese system actually has five elements that correspond to each of the organ meridian points as well as to stones or other materials that we energy healers might use to unblock them. These elements are:

Water: Water rules over the emotion of fear, just as it does in Western symbolism, and is represented best by blue or sea-green stones like Lapis Lazuli, Sodalite, Chalcedony, Celestite, or Fluorite. This element is connected to the meridians that run through our kidneys, bladder, and ears, as well as anything we might expressly associate with our bones. Where these paths may be concerned, you may also choose to use a water material like Coral or Pearl in lieu of a traditional crystal, and, of course, Quartz is always good.

Fire: Fire rules over the anxious emotions, those quick and potentially imprinting experiences we have when we feel panicked and out of control. It is best represented with red to brown stones like Lodestone, Bloodstone, Carnelian, Ruby, Jasper, Hematite, or even Jet or Lava Stones, given their origins. Fire is connected to the meridians that run through the tongue, heart, and small intestine and is also related to our blood and the arteries and veins that carry that blood throughout our bodies.

Metal: Metal doesn't typically show up as a separate element in Western traditions, but the diaspora of culture means you may find it melded with other elements or philosophies from other areas. Metal governs our grief and depressive emotions, those emotional states that lay us low and sap us of our energy. It can be simple to use actual metal in place of stones for this, such as copper pennies or even pieces of Meteorite or Lodestones. You can also use any black gemstone to represent this, such as

Obsidian or Onyx, or any stone that contains metal, such as
Lapis Lazuli, Iolite, Kunzite, or Labradorite. This element is
contained in the channels which pass through our nose, lungs,
and large intestine, and it governs the health of our skin, hair,
and nails.

Earth: Earth governs our sense of worry, or those times when
we are projecting a future which hasn't happened yet. As you
might imagine, this element is represented well by Green or
Brown stones like Emerald, Jade, Moss Agate, or Jasper. Earth
oversees the meridians that pass through the mouth, stomach,
and spleen and is called to aid us in afflictions of the muscles
and musculature.

Wood: Wood also does not appear as a separate element in
many Western traditions, but you may find it echoed in the
characters of Westernized Earth elements or as a separate entity
in traditions which hold to a World Tree, Tree of Life, or Tree
of Knowledge concept. This element oversees our emotional
experience of anger, the boiling rage or fury that can grow up
within us. Actual wood can work well as a stand-in for crystals in
this area, but we caution you to choose wood that is either alive
and still attached to the tree (like sitting beneath a living tree) or
twigs which have freely fallen from it rather than trying to cut a
branch yourself or using wood you find in a shop. You can also
use Petrified Wood or Jet, which is compressed wood, or you can
use amber, which is petrified sap from a tree. Wood governs the
meridians which pass through our eyes, liver, and gall bladder,
and it governs afflictions of the tendons, which stretch over and
around joints and joint points.

PALM POINTS

Receptive: The receptive palm point is connected to the Heart Chakra and relates to your experience of love, support, abundance, meeting the right people, and opening up to new achievements. It is an important portal to maintaining the balance of energy so you don't become drained. A blocked receptive palm point may mean you are rejecting help and support from those who love you or that you simply don't believe you are worthy of receiving that love and support. You may also be telling yourself you don't have enough time or energy in life or that you lack other critical resources (like money). In a blocked state, you will likely have trouble manifesting because you are removed from connecting to your goals through your heart and ability to receive. It may challenge you to love yourself fully, and you may find your inner voice saying things like *How could anyone love someone like me?* or *I'm not worthy of this experience.*

To make sure the receptive palm point stays open, it is helpful to acknowledge everything you accept and express gratitude for all you receive. It may be very simple. You can simply accept that water quenches your thirst and say "thank you" to that water for doing so. Or perhaps accept and thank a beautiful sunset, a hug from a friend, a pet's love, or the clothes you are wearing right now. Even when times are rough, you can accept the rough experience and try to find the lesson in it. Then, thank the rough time for the lesson. In no way are we suggesting that you ought to be grateful for rough times; rather, reframe your experience to think about something you *learned* from it, however marginal it may be, and focus on the gratitude for *that lesson* whenever you can instead of on the rough time. In this way, you can subtly move your experience from the loss to the gain by reframing your thoughts and the language you use when you "talk" to yourself about those thoughts. Try heart openers like Labradorite or Rose Quartz to help remove a blockage in a receptive palm point.

Dominant: The dominant palm point, also connected to the Heart, relates to your ability to give, express, declare, act, share, release, and create. If it is blocked, you may have difficulty letting go emotionally, sharing your emotions with others, or experiencing your own sense of agency as a creator of your own life and the events within it. You might be afraid of making waves or dragging others down with your emotions. Think of it as a pen in your hand with clogged ink. How can you draw up your plans, write a love letter, or even jot down your to-do list with a clogged pen? In this state, your energy flow is not effectively creating the best version of yourself; just like the pen, if you squeeze or shake too hard, you will explode. You need to ease yourself back into a smoothly flowing dominant palm point.

To keep this portal open, try this simple practice. Focus your attention on deliberately sending positive energy out into the world. It might be an intention to be kind to someone today, or you might send a gift to a friend in the mail or generously tip at your coffee shop. You can also use journaling or art to write affirmations, expressing a positive goal and what you need to plan, manifest, and process that goal. For a blocked dominant palm point, consider heart defenders, grounding or Root stones like Bloodstone, Carnelian, or Ruby, or manifesting Crown stones like Amethyst. Hold these stones to either Root or Crown and say, "I am safe." Then move the stone to your Heart and say, "I am loved." Repeat this action a few times, picking up speed as you go until you feel a circuit of energy forming through the action of moving the crystal up and down over your body in this way. When you feel that you are, in fact, safe and loved, slow your pace, let out a breath, and return your attention to your body. All will be well.

One of Lune's favorite practices for working on both the receptive and the dominant palm points is to take a Clear Quartz point and place it between both palms, as in prayer hands, with the base resting in the dominant palm and the terminated end directed into the receptive palm. In meditation or a relaxed state, fill your mind with images of love, support, abundance, laughter, excitement, and desires. Allow these images to invoke these feelings of joy, comfort, love, stability, and excitement within your heart. Feel the emotion growing within you and direct this feeling. Let it travel out your chest, into your dominant shoulder, down your arm, and out your dominant palm through the crystal and into the receptive palm, up the arm, into the shoulder and back into the heart. As you focus on creating this channel, allow phrases or mantras to assist you: *I have so much love to give. I accept all the support the Universe has to share. I create my life experience. I give generously. I receive in abundance.*

Another version of this same exercise is to use two Clear Quartz points, each held in the palm so that one point is facing outwards toward the fingertips of the dominant hand and the other is directed inward toward the wrist of the receptive one. Imagine they are arrows pointing outward and inward. You can focus again on being open to giving and receiving on behalf of your greatest good, as well as the greatest good of those around you. See yourself pulling everything you need in through your receptive palm's crystal to your heart with gratitude and sending out your best intentions through your dominant palm's crystal with love. If Quartz does not speak to you for this exercise, please feel free to use whatever stones resonate with you. What's most important is that the stones you use *work for you.* There is no "right stone" for this work.

JOINTS

Ankles

Metaphysically, ankles relate to your upbringing in general as well as how well supported you feel in your life, particularly by your family and friends. A blockage here may cause you to feel ungrounded or unsteady, as if you aren't very graceful or can't find your footing easily. This could be either metaphorically, like you are struggling to experience authenticity, or it may mean literally, like you are tripping over your shoes and the sidewalk curb. When the connections of this joint's energy to other energy centers is examined, you may also find that your Solar Plexus and Root Chakras are under-energized. As you seek to manifest stability, think about the different types of resources you may need: wellness practices and routines, friends who support you, or perhaps even money. Set aside a little fund without hoarding it; just place it somewhere it can serve your greatest good and gather more to itself to help you achieve a goal. No matter how modest or grand the fund, it will add to the energy of your personal foundation.

Focus on building a solid foundation so you may feel sure-footed as you navigate your path. A good way to do this is to locate a very large rock (perhaps one you find outside at a national park) that you can literally stand upon. Spread your feet about shoulder-width apart so you are truly balanced, and feel the rock beneath your feet. Rock gently from side to side, swaying to shift your weight from one foot to the other without lifting them so you can feel your body's weight on your feet. Tell yourself, "I feel the Earth beneath me. I am held up." Repeat this for three breaths. A variation of this exercise is to place a palm-sized rock under the arch of each foot while you stand barefoot on them inside your home. Good options for this are Lodestones, Geodes, Palm Selenite, Calcite, or any flat stone in a dark brown to red color.

Knees

The knee is associated with flexibility, bending, adaptability, and comfort with all of the above. In the ideal state, having balanced knees where the energy is flowing suggests you are open to change, whether to the plans you have for the day or what task to tick off your day's to-do list first. We are all best served by being flexible, because it is a good reminder that there is much outside of our own control. When we are too rigid with our expectations, we may change slowly and uncomfortably, kicking and screaming along the way. Rigidity is typically unnecessary and definitely not helpful to your stress level and personal vibration. Validate discomfort as needed for your awareness, but, after a few calming breaths, you are better served to set your intention to go with the flow. Simply declare aloud or internally, "I am open to going with the flow of the Universe. I trust that things will work out. I will be flexible with myself to harmonize with this flow, and things will begin working out for me."

An example of a knee energy blockage often occurs in clients who are very focused on manifesting a goal, such as attracting a romantic partner or increasing their income, but who are rigid in their ideas of how they will meet this person or obtain these funds. For example, maybe they're picturing a very specific person (never a good idea) for that true love or predict that a specific lottery ticket win will bring in those funds. Very commonly, blocked knee points pair with an over-energized Throat and/or Third Eye and can cause tunnel vision. Ocean Jasper and Larimar are excellent stones for surrendering to the flow. Whether worn in jewelry, kept as a pocket stone, or held in the hands during meditation, these stones must be set with an intention to begin opening paths for you which will lead you to your goal in comfort and ease. Remember to tell your stones to do the work you want them to do.

Hips

The hips tend to harbor heavy emotional weights or energetic burdens, such as anger, stress, or fear. Imagine you are wearing pants with large pockets that are filled to the brim with the objects of your day, only these objects are energetic "junk"; it would serve you better to just release them rather than to continue to feel limited by the weight in your pockets. Similar to the dominant palm point, heavy energy in the hips is stored in deposits that are not being released for a reason unique to the individual. Perhaps you don't want to "pollute" the atmosphere with the burden of your anger or stress. Perhaps you feel you really need to carry this weight by yourself, or that no one would help you anyway, so why bother? Others may hold onto the discomfort of a burdened hip point because they are more concerned about the discomfort they'll feel if they actually face what they carry there, as if they are breathing life into these burdens. These burdens are emotional weights that you have been repressing in some way, and now they are manifesting in your hips and low back. Ever had a "pain in the butt?" That's probably a hip blockage (and we all know it's those closest relationships that at times get labeled as a "pain in the butt"). It is also possible you don't want to release the blockage because you feel it serves to protect you—after all, that hip pain or abdominal tightness reminds you that you are strong, you can move, and you can step aside. Maybe you need this to keep others distant or protect yourself from actions you are afraid will make these areas hurt even worse.

Moving the hips is a great way to keep the energy flowing through the meridians here. Whether you enjoy dancing, walking, or hip opening poses in yoga, moving your hips with the focus and intention of releasing stored emotional burdens or energy blockages is quite effective. Take deep yet comfortable breaths, and, as you exhale, send the exhalation either via your will or your declaration to the hips as they shake and shimmy and sway. While your hips sway in a gentle circle, imagine the stress and fear you feel shaking out the sides like ruffles on a skirt that bounce when you dance. Just feel it shake loose to serve your best outcome.

Gemstones such as Smoky Quartz, Brecciated Jasper, Bloodstone, or Tree Agate are very supportive of keeping the hips in a balanced state when paired with intention to release these emotional burdens.

A beaded belt of Jasper or Bloodstone is not only a fetching accessory, it's also a hip point activator. Just drape the chain of stones loosely over your hips before you begin dancing. Speak your intentions to the stones in the belt, and start moving.

Elbow

Like the knees, elbows relate to our ability to handle change, but, in this case, it's more about our ability to adapt to our own progress or development. If the knees link more to adaptability to the path itself, as the knees serve the function of moving our feet along the path, then the elbow represents how comfortable we are with our own inner or external changes as we go—aesthetic adjustments as well as the more nurturing changes we employ. Changing careers, rewriting our story, moving beyond who we used to be, and acting from the place of an enhanced version of ourselves all happen at the elbows. This is often seen paired with an imbalance in the Heart Chakra and/or the Solar Plexus.

As we move through life, you must take charge of who you are becoming. It is only you who can adjust the dynamic of your *Self*, through enforcing your personal boundaries, making choices for yourself, planting your seeds, and allowing your energy to flow in the direction of your choosing. Again, journaling is very helpful for becoming more comfortable with stepping into the greatest version of who you can be. Writing is a powerful act of creation. Manifest all you deserve and desire with these affirmations in your journal: "I am empowered, confident, fair and just, compassionate, wealthy, generous, loved and loving, supported, organized, graceful, and patient."

Shoulder

The shoulders, like the hips, are a place where we carry weights. These can be many things unique to each of us, but they often include family obligations, unwanted projects (like work projects or favors), or qualities we've taken on which don't necessarily serve us (like "being the rock of the family"). We all have our roles, but our shoulders can take on the baggage of these roles and pull you down. A common shoulder complaint, for instance, is pain related to typing too often at a traditional computer or laptop, from holding a driving wheel to drive long distances, or from carrying a diaper bag or an overstuffed handbag across the shoulders. In each of these cases, the relationship to the shoulder is clear: it is the upholder of our work, our creative processing, our obligations to our families, and our travel. Relieving the shoulders often begins by determining if the object or action is truly necessary for your greatest good (like, do you really need your partner's rock collection in your diaper bag? Do you really need your steering wheel to be up that high?).

If you find that you do need these things, then it's time to relax this zone by doing some basic stretches. Bring your shoulders up to your ears and hold them for a breath. Then, push them down as though the blades are sliding down your back. Repeat: up and then down. Now roll them forward and backward to release the tension. Because the shoulders reside between the Heart and Throat, it is a good idea to determine if the Heart and Throat are under or over-energized. Using the color system as a guideline, very often we will find the Throat Chakra in an over-energized state and the Heart under-energized. This can feel like a literal weight on your shoulders.

As you can imagine, when the Throat is over-energized, we feel very much "in our heads" and burdened by what ifs and other disempowering thoughts, as well as the never-ending to-do list we might constantly be reminding ourselves about. You can use stones to release this hyperactive mental state, such as peachy, pink, or soft violet stones (Morganite, Pink Fluorite, or Lepidolite) which often have an excellent effect on the shoulders. When the Heart is in an under-energized state, we often are missing the messages of our own truest desires, so there is a greater potential to carry a burden for others' causes.

Stones such as Rhodonite, Chrysoprase, and Moss or Tree Agate are excellent for working with the Heart space. They help to heal unworthiness, guilt, or self-criticism, and they also strengthen one's awareness of one's personal desires so we more easily can identify when something is not for us and let it go. Do you feel a release of tension? Ask your stone, "What can I let go of? What can I drop?" Because the shoulders have to do with the weight of the things we are carrying inside or in our arms and hands, it is important to know what you really need to hold onto and what can be released. So ask. You may be surprised by the result. Breathe into your chest and notice how your shoulders pull back when your lungs expand. With a crystal in each hand, hold your hands skyward in yoga's "Sun Salutation" pose to both stretch the shoulders and release them.

Neck

The neck is a point that is sometimes conflated with the shoulders because they are often experienced together. A stiffness in the neck is often felt in the shoulders, or shoulder pain may limit the mobility of the neck. Thus, a neck that is unable to fully twist side to side is now supporting a head that can't see clearly in all directions. It's literally blocking one's vision. Likewise, shoulders that are so tense as to stiffen a neck's joint point could make it hard to breathe or speak easily, and that may mean a poor sense of security on the physical level. Also, on the emotional and spiritual levels, this may mean an inability to become inspired or to move others to inspiration by your spoken words. It may mean you are also swallowing down more than you can chew, either literally with food choices or perhaps with substances like drugs or alcohol as ineffective coping skills, or figuratively with projects, agreements, or commitments that overextend your typical workday.

When the neck is blocked, the release methods almost always include some form of clear communication, whether that is setting a clear boundary, owning up to a miscommunication or misunderstanding, or clearing the air after a fight. You can employ any blue stone for neck work, including Sapphire, Sodalite, Lapis Lazuli, Aquamarine, Rainbow Moonstone, Fluorite, Celestite, and really any other stone that speaks to you. The neck is the perfect place to wear a necklace to keep this energy flowing openly all day long, but if you are not inclined to wear jewelry, consider other options. You can use a Fluorite point to direct energy like an arrow or wand that you point to direct the energy to flow from one place to the other. You might take a palm-sized Celestine and press it to your throat before you make a phone call to a coworker or friend with whom you need to set clear expectations or boundaries. Release the neck point with calm purpose and direction. You will be understood.

Imagine a line from the back of your neck at the top of your spine moving up the back of the skull: This location is often associated with the Zeal Chakra, also known as the "mouth of God" point. You can picture this area as the "back of the mind," and it can often harbor memories or elements we have "pushed to the back" for one reason or another. Sometimes it is out of necessity, if we are unprepared to fully process an experience and just need a little time to gather resources. Other times, what we stow away are elements of ourselves that we may have repressed for one reason or another: it might be an artistic ability, the desire to become a parent, or a longing to travel. This is a space of our present belief systems, patterns, and what we think we know. When there is evidence of a need to release a thought pattern or limiting belief system, then working with the back of the neck and lower skull can be quite powerful. Stones which access this field are Kambaba Stone and Eudialyte. Simply setting an intention into a stone to help you release that which does not serve you or limits you in any way and then placing either one under your pillow as you rest can relieve a blocked Zeal chakra.

The base of the neck and down into the space between the shoulder blades is an area related to your outer "shell." Another way to envision this space is as a cape, or something we "wear." This area comes up often in healing sessions when a person is in a time of transformation, like a butterfly wiggling out of a cocoon. Even if it is unnoticed and you don't think there is an issue here, it can be helpful to the process of your personal transformation to sit with and tend to this space with mindfulness and meditation. An ideal way to support this area is to take a warm salt bath with clay and gemstones such as Snowflake Obsidian, African Turquoise (Jasper), or Quartz with Phantom or Garden formations.

WORKING WITH THE FULL BODY'S MERIDIANS

Bath Rituals

Sacred baths are a beautiful way to weave together self-care, relaxation, and your own divine intentions. They not only cleanse your energy, but they also provide a metaphorical rebirth into a new phase of your life experience or your own personal development. As with most rituals, you should bring into them anything symbolic to your personal journey to accompany the stones or crystals you select. If nothing comes immediately to your mind, consider the four or five elements.

Each of the elements represents a different microcosmic experience
at a macrocosmic scale. Earth in the microcosm is your body in
relation to the macrocosm of the planet Earth. It literally supports
you as you take each step, and the food it creates through farming and
agriculture also supports your body. You bring this into your ritual
work by way of the crystals or stones you choose to ground you and
symbolize your connection to the physical plane. Microcosmically,
water is your blood, and macrocosmically it is the network of seas
and rivers that traverse the planet. Draw this element into your
ritual through the bath water itself or essential oils to represent
your emotions and the act of cleansing. Air is our breath in the
microcosm and air itself, or the winds that blow new possibilities into
our lives, in the macrocosm. The smoke from incense symbolizes
the mental plane of ideas and words. If you cannot tolerate smoke,
no matter—air is all around us, so just take a moment to tune into
your breath. Fire is the energy of life, as electrical impulses are what
power the body microcosmically, and that same energy at a larger
scale idealized as Spirit or Soul is the macrocosmic version of that
energy. A candle flame symbolizes the power of transformation and
rapid cleansing. You might also choose a religious symbol or a work
of art to bring into the experience. The important part is what you
apply to it. Fire and Metal can represent spirit or soul, and the flame
can symbolize the cause and effect path of choice and the power of
thought and action to make changes in the world around us. And
don't forget—each of the elements can be symbolized by a crystal
or a stone to stand in its place. You might choose a Lava Stone or a
bright red Ruby to represent fire, for instance, or a Pearl or pale blue
Aquamarine to represent water.

~~~~~~~~~~~~~~~~~~~~~~~~~~~~~~~~~~~~~

Sound Baths:

A sound bath is a healing session with a shamanic or light working
practitioner or on your own. These sessions work well with a Selenite

Wand to gently brush the aura as if you are using the wand to comb through your subtle body (about six inches from your actual body). To perform a sound bath, you might elect to use Tibetan bells (which require a lot of concentration to chime), clinking them together and listening to the sound until you can no longer hear the reverberation. You could choose a tuning fork or Tibetan singing bowl; singing bowls come in metal or crystal. Chime the tuning fork or bowl and then move it near the side of your head to absorb the vibrations. You can also gently strike a bowl to make it sound and resonate like a gong and place it on your body while you are resting on your back. Center it on one of your chakra points for added effect. And, of course, you can always pop in a pair of ear buds and tune into some cleansing sounds, such as one of Lune Innate's sound healing videos.

Water Intention Baths:

To get started with a water bath ritual, bring the four elements of Earth, Air, Fire, and Water into your bathroom. You might consider a candle, incense, crystal or stone, essential oil, and a piece of gold jewelry. White candles are ideal as they include the vibrations of all the colors at once and represent pure light. Incense of any kind will do, but white sage is ideal for clearing "negative" energy. Clear Quartz, the Master Healer, is a great crystal with no risk of dissolving in water if you choose to submerge it. You could also place Black or Blue Kyanite nearby (but do not submerge them). A chunk of Pink Salt (Lune's favorite) can be added to the water directly to create a soft salt bath, and a good-sized chunk may last several sessions. Lavender essential oil is a good bathwater addition for peace and tranquility, and Frankincense is a nice addition to honor the divine work of your personal path. Gold is an ideal metal if you choose to add this fifth element to your process because it is not corroded by water. What you include is your choice, and whatever you bring into this ritual space should be personally meaningful to you. Just please remember that some essential oils can cause reactions and skin eruptions, some stones are toxic, others will dissolve in water, and some metals rust or corrode, so do your research before putting anything into a tub with you.

As your bath fills, light your candle and set an intention. You might say something aloud like, "On behalf of my highest and greatest good and in perfect comfort and alignment, it is my will and intention to hold space in this sacred bath ritual for the purpose of clearing all energy which does not support me, to release what no longer serves me, and to clear projections and energies directed to me by others which do not support my desires and overall wellness." Next, light your incense and add a few drops of essential oil to your bath water. Place your crystal and metal near the water alongside the candle and incense. Be careful not to put your crystal in the water unless you are absolutely certain it is nontoxic and not water-soluble. Try keeping a collection of salt chunks to add directly to your bath water as Lune does. They dissolve in warm water and add a purifying crystal element. Epsom or bath salt is another crystal alternative.

Holding your intention clearly in your mind, step into your bath and savor the sensations of it. Really enjoy it. Remember to rinse off when you are done, particularly if you added salt or oil to your water. As you finish, declare your work with a definitive statement, such as "And so it is" or "Manifest my Will," or any other statement with similar concluding sentiment. The goal is to use that declaration to conclude your energetic work.

~~~~~~

Water Healing or Manifestation Bath:

A similar process to the Water Intention Bath can be used to heal yourself, to initiate yourself into a new process for personal development, or to manifest a goal or outcome. Follow the same steps to set up your water as you did with the previous exercise. Select your candle in accordance with what you are working toward by color, scent, or both, keeping in mind what these qualities symbolize to you. If this is a bath to heal heartache, perhaps a rose-scented pink or green candle will help you tune into your Heart Center. If you are looking to manifest creative channeling into your persona or you wish to support a project you are tackling, you might select a gold, orange, or yellow candle. You may take guidance from the chakras and their corresponding colors or else just let your intuition guide you. Select your incense, oil, and gemstone in the same manner—whatever might support your present intention, such as Rose and Rose Quartz for healing heartache, or Citrus and Carnelian for creative energy.

Just as before, speak your intention as the water fills. You might say something like, "On behalf of the highest and greatest good, in perfect comfort and alignment, it is my will and intention for this sacred bath to support my heart healing. Identify the lesson and growth in the experience. Guide me toward my heart's fulfillment."

If you do not have access to a bathtub, you can easily modify this exercise for a standing shower. Araminta often hangs a sachet filled with herbs and crystals from her shower head when she does not have time for a full bath ritual. Alternatively, you could add these to a water bowl for a face-cleansing exercise, or even do it over the sink. It is your *intention* that matters here more than the tools you use to accomplish it.

PROJECTIONS

In the more subtle space of the energetic body—sometimes called "the auric layer" or the "etheric membrane," for example—there tends to be an area along the back of the body in general where our projections collect. Projections are essentially thoughts, assumptions,

or internal wishes that are directed toward you by another person.
You can also send your own projections out to those around you.
Often, it is a well-intended sending by a friend or family member
who thinks they know what is best for you or only wants you to be
happy, but their definition of "happy" or what they believe would
make you happy may not align with your personal truth. We often see
this with parents and children, where perhaps a mother may believe
her daughter will only be happy when she settles down and becomes
a mother or marries a doctor or grows to become one herself. The
problem is that this belief may not be anything close to what her
daughter might enjoy. Instead, the daughter may have no desire to
become a parent and finds her fulfillment in traveling to new places.
It is not that the mother is wishing ill on her daughter, but she isn't
exactly helping either. While there is some truth in the phrase "what
other people think of you has nothing to do with you," there is a
risk. These thoughts sent from mother to daughter or really from any
person to another risk being concentrated and may accumulate into
a kind of fog or confusion. We can carry with us the expectations of
others to the point that we develop a shield between our authentic
selves and the will of the world.

If the energy of the projection is not cleared, then a person will likely
come to a crossroads where they must choose between their authentic
self and the expectations of someone else. Going back to our original
example, imagine that the daughter may begin to doubt her truth and
question if her lifestyle is somehow "wrong" or inappropriate in some
way. The resonance or energetic field of a projection, too, represents
the within and without principle also stated in the ancient aphorism,
"As above so below." The concept here is that what we imagine will
happen is what we manifest through choices and actions, and vice
versa. What we experience outside is repeated inside, such as through
thoughts and emotions. In this example, that contradicting layer could
begin to cloud the authentic energy of the daughter, and then other

people in her life may begin to perceive her as unsure or confused, and this will only increase that discord energy.

Another example is in the way that our assumptions can feed off each other, even though they are often based on a very limited perspective. For example, if you run into someone who has a cold and then, the next time you see them, they have bad allergies or a sprained foot, you might begin to assume that they are sickly or have bad luck with their physical vitality. Even if that were the case, by seeing them as "sick," we hold them in that state and send more of that energy to them through projection. It would be much more helpful to the individual if we saw them as building up their inner strength or immunity instead of seeing them as unwell. This is why it is so important to mind the soapbox. Share your challenges with those whom you know will hold you in a state of wellness and accomplishment and not a state of pity or weakness. While you do need to be heard and validated, you must also protect your personal energy. Social media has made it far too easy to quickly share our struggles with hundreds of people in an instant. There is such a beauty to vulnerability and sharing our stories with others, but you must do so thoughtfully and take care to cleanse yourself of projections on a regular basis. Baths, sound healing, Reiki, spiritual cleansing, Selenite wands, float tanks, and so on are all wonderful to do this. Stones which support protecting the energetic field are Fluorite and aura-treated stones such as Aqua Aura Quartz, Pyrite, or Hematite.

THE GIFT OF STONES EXERCISE

Energy does not like to be stagnant, and, in fact, many esoteric teachings define "evil" as stagnation. Everything changes, and surrendering to change that serves you can be both liberating and positive. Energy ebbs and flows, and it gives and receives. All energy can be said to move along a spectrum from feminine to masculine, positive to negative, and receptive to active, which are all expressions of the hermetic law of rhythm. You likely feel uncomfortable when you are "stuck" in a stagnating situation where you either can't or won't go with the flow of energy. Growing and changing is necessary to wellness and overall comfort, but it's important to remember that rest is not the same as stagnation. Stagnation occurs when you *resist* change, but rest occurs when you embrace the pauses that are necessary to action. Even sadness and grief have the potential to give rise to massive personal growth and empathy. Similarly, a person only learns something new in a state of moderate discomfort or in the zone where the skill she is developing exists in proximity to need (discomfort) and the "next level up" (ability), because it is that emotional experience that prompts us to develop a skill or ability in the first place. This polarity or perhaps the spectrum between need and achievement is demonstrated in the tarot deck by the Death card, which is more accurately interpreted as the ending of one cycle and the birth of a new one, or perhaps a transformation. This crystal exercise is a great tool for letting go, giving back, and developing all at the same time. It is a great action to take to both give and receive.

Select a stone that you cherish, but not one you will sorely miss if you no longer possess it. It is important, however, that this stone is one you personally value, as you are about to gift this stone to someone else. You might actually begin to collect or purchase small stones specifically for the purposes of sharing them with others. These can be ones you collect on a beach or walk, the polished river stones you can typically buy at a craft store, or stones that you have yourself received as gifts. If you shop online for crystals, some vendors will include extras as gifts to you, such as tiny Quartz points, and you might set these aside for this exercise. If you know you are going to be visiting a place where you can collect stones, such as a riverbank or a nature trail, gather some up for this gift-exercise.

Now, plan to go into a public space with the intention of giving this stone and its energy to the world around you. Hold the energy in your hands and fill it with affirmations. You might speak these directly into the stone in your hands so that your breath moves over its surface, or you can simply imagine affirmative, positive messages. These can include anything you would wish to hear yourself or messages to encourage someone else, and particularly words that resonate with the type of stone you have selected. These might include "Love, heal, and rejoice" for a piece of Rose Quartz, "See what's ahead of you and trust your intuition" for a polished Tiger's Eye, or "Know you are safe and stable, and feel the grounding influence of the abundance that surrounds you" for a piece of Bloodstone or Raw Ruby.

Choose a place to take this stone where you know other people are likely to visit. This might be a beach walk at sunset, a nature trail at a nearby conservancy, or a public park or playground. Head to this place with the stone in your hand. As you walk or sit on a park bench, really imagine someone coming along and finding your stone. See the delight she will experience when she catches sight of it and adds it to her pocket. Visualize the affirmation you set into the stone washing over her as an extension of your good will. Now leave the stone in plain sight and walk away. This is now your gift to the next traveler who needs a crystal pick-me-up.

One variation of this activity is to bring a pocket full of stones and, like Hansel and Gretel, make your crystal gift as a path. By offering a mini trail of stones to the next passersby, you may be gifting more than one person, or you may be offering the subconscious, spiritual support of providing a direction to someone else who might benefit from taking some of the same steps you have. A variation of this exercise that Araminta likes to do when she's feeling low is to also empty her pockets of any loose change she has in them. Just imagining the joy a child experiences when he finds a fistful of shiny quarters on the sidewalk is enough to lift her own spirits, and nearly all children have had a rock collection in their lifetimes, too. As you go about your journey, use your dominant hand (the hand you use to write) to place the stones where you feel guided to leave them. Focus on feeling generous and sharing with others. Feel how good it is to pass on beautiful things, to release what you don't necessarily need that might support someone else or lighten someone's day. Who doesn't love to find a little hidden treasure in the weeds?

If you spot a stone in the wild yourself, don't be afraid to collect it if you are in a place where you know it is acceptable to do so. Be sure to express your gratitude for the experience. Hold the stones in your receptive hand (your left, if you are right-handed) and think about three things for which you feel grateful. You might choose to recall a treasured experience, a connection, a hug, a starry night, your family, or your home. Be grateful for the water in your cup, the air you breathe, or the music to which you are listening. As you receive your stone gift, express thanks. If you mind wanders to less pleasant experiences while expressing gratitude within yourself, guide it back.

SUPPORTING OTHERS WITH CRYSTAL HEALING

There may be some occasions where you provide a healing experience to another person like a client or a friend, or where you have someone present who can assist you in healing yourself by placing stones on your body for you. We have already described the process of holding an amplifying stone, such as Quartz, in your receptive hand to energize the Qi coming into your body and a releasing stone, such as Jet, in your dominant hand, to disperse and release the energy you expel from your body. In addition to this, we recommend placing stones along the center of the body or at the major joint points. If you (or the other person) are face down, place stones along the spine and then at the major joint points, including the elbows, hips, and knees. If you can't balance a stone on the body, just place the stone on the table or bed beside the person or ask your helper to do the same. You may choose stones that relate to the traditional elements of the meridians in Chinese medicine (Water, Fire, Earth, Metal, and Wood) and align these elemental stones with the organs in the body through which the meridian flows most strongly. You may also choose to use only amplifiers, like Quartz Crystals, or to mix and match the chakra system with your meridian work and use a rainbow of stones along the spine from the head to the pelvis. Remember, if you're not sure what to do, you can always dowse or muscle test to ask yourself and your intuition what you truly feel is best. The answers are within you.

Once the stones are placed, rub your hands together to generate heat from the friction. This action should be brisk, as the act itself calls on fire and manifestation because you are literally moving quickly when you do this. Rubbing your hands together in this way is an excellent step in the manifestation process, as it generates action. Once your hands are sufficiently warmed, gently place them on each joint point. If the joint point does have a stone on it, just place your warmed hand over the stone so it covers the stone and overlaps it.

Please note that if you are practicing this with someone else, it is essential that you ask permission before touching anyone on any part of their body! Healing does not work when it is uninvited or uncomfortable, so you must request clear consent from the person you are working with. And that's not all: when you place your hands on another person, you do put them at risk. What if you slip? What if you press too hard? What if they misinterpret your action or are triggered by it into a sense of discomfort? If you are going to work with another person, we strongly encourage you to pursue certification and liability insurance, as well as to read up on the governing practices for energy healers (which are sometimes nestled within massage therapist regulations) for your state, province, or country. If you are unsure of the rules or just don't want to risk it, you can also generate an energetic flow by rubbing your hands briskly together and holding them twelve inches or so above the body—but remember to ask permission first! Even this act of non-touch can trigger someone. The goal here is healing and relaxation, so the last thing we wish to do is cause harm during a healing session.

Finally, it is worth reminding you that this chapter is meant as a general guide and by no means encompasses all the elements of working with meridians or Traditional Chinese Medicine. True Chinese medicine is a labor-intensive practice which includes years of academic and clinical study and board examinations for licensure, as it is a medical practice. We offer this chapter to get you warmed up to a much larger topic and to provide you with different places in the body where you might focus your crystal energies differently and to great effect.

CHAPTER 9

CRYSTALS AND THE ZODIAC

By now you have established a good understanding that crystal healing allows you to harness the peaceful, viriditas or "greening" energy of stones and minerals to develop your own personalized sense of wellness. One way to apply these energetic principles of crystal healing is to integrate your work with other planetary principles, such as working with crystals at a particular time of day, phase of the Moon, ebb and flow of the tide, turn of the season, or passage of constellations across the night sky. For the purposes of this chapter, we will use the Western Zodiac as opposed to the Vedic Zodiac, which offers slightly different mathematical methods of calculating which of the twelve astrological constellations may have been over you at the time of your birth. The simplified Western Zodiac offers a fixed date range for figuring out which is your Sun Sign, and this primary sign describes a potential personality type that you can use to align crystals with your wellness journey. While this chapter details crystals and stones you might use for your specific Sun Sign, it is important to remember that you can benefit from any stone and that you are not limited to working with stones that correspond to your natal chart (or birth chart).

For example, if your birthday is August 16, then according to the Western Zodiac, your Sun Sign is Leo. Perhaps one day, though, you find yourself with far too much work to complete in the eight-hour day you have at the office and would like to tap into the energy of a stabilizing or "get the job done" sign such as Capricorn. You can easily do this by wearing or meditating with stones associated with that sign. Or you may prefer to relax that energy and let go of some of the extra work that has been loaded onto your shoulders.

You might then decide to attract the energy of a more fluid sign, such as Cancer, and you could use the stones associated with that sign to do so.

Another way to look at Zodiac stones is to consider which sign of the Zodiac is dominant in your *present moment*. For example, when the Sun is in Pisces (between February 18 and March 20), you may find yourself very sensitive, emotional, and lethargic as that Piscean energy influences everything around you. In this state, you may wish to draw in a complementary energy, such as the grounded and supportive Earth energy of Virgo. You might choose stones related to Virgo to help you ground during this time, or you may find you prefer to use the Piscean period of the calendar to explore emotions you've been putting aside or bottling up. In that case, you'd pull out the crystals and stones related to Pisces.

As a whole, crystal healing and other metaphysical arts such as astrology or chakra balancing (as we've previously described) are intuitive processes. Rely on your intuition as you use stones to create harmony and intention in your daily wellness practice. We hope you are beginning to see these gifts from Mother Earth as not just beautiful tools, but also as helpers with their own unique personalities. By no means is this an exhaustive list of correspondences, and really no stone "belongs" to a specific sign, but it can be helpful to imagine that your stones and your stars really do have personalities, even if you decide for yourself what they are. Given that each astrological sign also has a kind of personality, we have offered this list as a suggestion for how you might incorporate your intuition, intention, and meaning into your work with gemstones and the movement of the stars.

To get started, most Western Zodiac charts begin with the sign of Aries, as it occurs during the Spring or Vernal Equinox, marking the end of winter and the beginning of growth. We will start there as well.

Each sign is outlined here with a brief description of the sign itself, and then the elements, chakras, paths, opposite signs, and potential crystals with similar personalities that correspond with it. The *Higher Path* section refers to the type of energy most often associated with this sign, and, therefore, it describes the sign's individual strengths, which can be leveraged to achieve personal growth in those areas. The *Lower Path* represents the shadow or the particular weaknesses of the sign which may need to be processed and transmuted, or at least honored and compassionately acknowledged while working toward personal growth. Stones can be used to either augment a *Higher Path* or cushion and transform a *Lower Path*.

ARIES (MARCH 20-APRIL 20)

Aries, or the starry constellation of The Ram, is ruled by the Roman God of War and that deity's associated planet, Mars.

Element: Fire

Chakras: Sacral, Solar Plexus, Heart, and Throat

Higher Path: Lots of creative energy, new ideas, and self-awareness

Lower Path: Impulsive, reactionary, aggressive

Opposite sign: Libra

Stones for Aries: Terminated Clear Quartz, Fire Quartz, Fire Agate, Super Seven, and Rainbow Obsidian

Aries has an almost rocket-like energy, infused with determination, focus, and the overall spark of life. Since it is a fire sign, stones may work well with candles flickering over them as you infuse them with intention. Gemstones with directional terminations, such as Quartz points, are ideal to use with Aries's arrow-like energy because you can use the termination like a laser beam to direct your intentions outward from yourself. Hold the stone in your hands while you focus on your intention or desire. Point the terminated end outward—either at the sky, the ground, or around you: anywhere not pointed inward toward your body. Then, draw yourself up with confidence and use your willpower to firmly declare your intention. Imagine your declaration is a ray of pure light flowing from you as its source out through the stone's pointed end toward the universe, amplified by the disposition of the Quartz point.

Stones with fiery flashes like Fire Agate and Rainbow Obsidian ignite the spark of creative energy, new ideas, and problem-solving. Alternatively, high vibrational stones like the composite known as Super Seven will lend your Aries-focused crystal healing an exciting, high-energy vibration. Sometimes, though, the high energy of Aries needs to be balanced. If you find you need to reduce aggression and hyperactivity, have a look at the suggested stones under Aries's opposite sign of Libra.

 ## TAURUS (APRIL 21–MAY 21)

The constellation of Taurus resembles the Bull, and it is ruled by the Roman Goddess of Love and her planet, Venus.

Element: Earth

Chakras: Root, Sacral, and Heart

Higher Path: Grounded and authentic, stable, romantic, luxurious, and sensual

Lower Path: Stubborn, over-indulgent (particularly with regard to sensuality), and lustful

Opposite Sign: Scorpio

Stones for Taurus: Kambaba Stone, Smoky Quartz, Tiffany Stone, Star Ruby, Amethyst, and Green Tourmaline

Taureans are well known for their deep connection with their senses as well as their ability to ground themselves in authenticity and luxury. Stones and crystal healing to attract that Taurus energy tend to tap into those Earthy qualities of love and stability. Kambaba invokes the energy of Taurus with its lush and fertile nature, while Smoky Quartz has a comfortable and homelike vibe. Star Ruby adds a sparkly eye-catching element to its assistance with the intention to ground. Tiffany Stone, also known as Opalized Fluorite, has a soft yet powerful energy, almost like the Queen or Empress cards in the Tarot. This stone helps to focus and attract a grounded, down-to-earth kind of love and romance—not the kind of head-in-the-clouds, short burst romances depicted in films, but rather the more mature, long-term and nurturing love intrinsic. Amethyst is said to amplify almost any purpose, and, when aligned with Taurus' higher path, this stone can help you to focus on your sense of purpose and prioritize your self-care. Green Tourmaline is a powerful Heart activator. It works to enhance your connection to your heart-based desires for authentic experience, creation, and expression.

If you find yourself being overly indulgent—perhaps you are eating or sleeping more than you'd like or more than you think is personally healthy—it can be helpful to draw in the energy of Scorpio to balance that Taurean desire to occupy and satisfy the senses. Because the Taurus energy and its stones are so grounded, it can also be stiflingly stubborn, with its hooves digging firmly into the ground against the flow of energy. Release work, or mindfulness activities that target "letting go" and "going with the flow" can be very useful for this Taurus energy, and tapping into the Scorpio stones and crystal healing work can balance that rigid teeter-totter.

GEMINI (MAY 21–JUNE 21)

The sign of Gemini resembles a pair of twin humans—specifically Castor and Pollux of Greek myth. This sign is ruled by the Roman God of Communication and Transition and the planet dedicated to this deity, Mercury.

Element: Air

Chakras: Sacral, Throat, and Third Eye

Higher Path: Comprehension, mastery of duality, clear communication, and ability to provide a "witnessing" perspective

Lower Path: Contradiction, overthinking, manipulation of others, or lying and/or transience

Opposite Sign: Sagittarius

Stones for Gemini: Lapis Lazuli, Azurite, Sodalite, Blue Fluorite, Moldavite, and Herkimer Diamond

Gemini energy is renowned for its ability to transition between things very quickly. Mercury is the closest planet to the sun, and, therefore, it appears to observers to move back and forth across the sky very quickly. The myths of the God for whom this planet is named describe a personality that doesn't believe in boundaries and can itself become a different being with very little effort. Of course, the cost of such a transient nature is an inability to ground and feel securely connected. Because Herkimer Diamonds are often double-terminated, with points on both ends creating a "twin" or back-and-forth energy field, these stones are easily associated with the mirror-like qualities of Gemini. Likewise, communication is key, and thus the blue, communication-chakra stones of Lapis Lazuli, Azurite, and Sodalite all support expression, communication, and the "lower mind" or Conscious Mind, also known as "the mind of this lifetime."

Blue Fluorite can help you to organize your thoughts and ease decision-making. Because the Gemini energy is so airy, like a kite floating aimlessly in the sky, the very grounding and Earthy practice of making decisions can be challenging. Hold a piece of Blue Fluorite against your throat. Before you let it touch your skin, ask it to help you communicate your personal truth and to know the truth wholly and fully before you speak. This crystal intention helps you to organize your words, and it can serve as a reminder of your desire to seek and experience truth. That simple crystal-process can be all it takes to frame your decisions and clarify which side of a choice you truly want for yourself.

Moldavite, which is actually a naturally occurring glass created by or within a meteor, can enhance your communication with your Higher Self or *Innate Mind.* Hold a piece of Moldavite against your forehead or in your hands and ask it to organize your *thoughts* as truthfully and authentically as possible. Refer to the stone multiple times throughout the day (perhaps by setting a timer as a reminder). Use it to check in with your thoughts. Are you on the track you want to pursue? If not, it's time for a mid-course correction.

CANCER (JUNE 21–JULY 22)

Cancer's constellation resembles the Crab, and it is ruled by the Moon. In Greek mythology, the Moon is a representation of the happily unwed goddess Artemis, the Huntress of the forest.

Element: Water

Chakras: Root, Heart, Third Eye, and Crown

Higher Path: Nurturing, emotional maturity, and healing of self and others

Lower Path: Hyperemotional, or histrionic, moody, and needy

Opposite sign: Capricorn

Stones for Cancers: Moonstone, Opal, Chrysoprase, Labradorite, Pink Agate, Larimar, and Aquamarine

Cancer energy is thought to be emotionally nourishing, empathetic, and tender. The stones associated with Cancer evoke an almost maternal vibration, akin to that loving, guiding, spiritual experience that supports us as we grow. Moonstone and Labradorite are both feldspars and have an energy which is softly mystic. They gently work to support the intuition or your ability to "read between the lines." Because Moonstone is aligned with the intuitive nature of the Moon, it is said to attract your soul mates when worn on your body and observed by others. Set an intention into your Moonstone to help you attract kindred spirits or soul mates (not necessarily the kind who become romantic partners, though that's okay too. We're talking about people fit for any kind of meaningful relationship, whether it be as friends, as mentors/mentees, or as love interests). As you wear this stone, pay close attention to the people who remark on it throughout the day. That opalescent sheen that flickers across a polished Moonstone is bound to get someone's attention, and the intention you set will help you to identify the people who might become lasting friends. When someone remarks on your Moonstone, tell them this significance and offer a conversation which will help the relationship manifest in a more tangible way. Repeat this exercise to surround yourself with a loving and supportive community.

In addition to the sparkly Moonstone and Labradorite stones for love and affection, Opal and Larimar both have a watery nature and support peace and compassion. Pink Agate, sometimes known as the "caregiver stone," develops patience and supports self-reflection. Use Pink Agate to draw on the Cancer quality of taking a moment to breathe before reacting. Hold it for three cleansing breaths, project your thoughts or emotions into the stone, and then feel reactivity melt away so that you can *respond* instead of *react* to the situation at hand. Aquamarine is an option to support emotional maturity and competency, helping you to validate your experiences but not attach to them. Use Aquamarine to meditate on your feelings. Ask it to help you understand your emotions and how you can use those emotions to most effectively guide you to your highest good.

Most of the stones outlined in this section are connected to intuition and emotion. But if you find yourself flooded by emotion, then drawing on Cancer energy may not be the best way for you to handle your situation. You can call on its grounding, opposite energy with Capricorn stones. Another option is containing the emotions within a stone box. You might choose a small Obsidian box, as this stone is well known to work as a shield between energies. Simply write the overwhelming emotion on a slip of paper and tuck it into your box. When you are ready to process that emotion, pull it out and work through it as needed. This grounding activity amplifies your ability to experience emotions in a healthy way by allowing you to "right-size" your experience and process those Cancerian energies on your own terms.

LEO (JULY 23–AUGUST 22)

The sign of Leo is a constellation of stars that resemble the Lion. This sign is ruled by the Sun and is associated with the Greek God Apollo, the Radiant One.

Element: Fire

Chakras: Root, Solar Plexus, and Throat

Higher Path: Courage, showmanship, love of self, self-confidence, and an energy of traditions and family values

Lower Path: Abrasive, egocentric, and easily damaged

Opposite sign: Aquarius

Stones for Leo: Tiger's Eye, Golden Apatite, Sunstone, Citrine, and Gold

Like the Sun that governs this sign, Leo energy is radiant, confident, and bold. The Leo vibration can boost your energy to get through an important work meeting or presentation, or it can supply the courage to finally ask that person you see in the elevator every day out for a coffee. Tiger's Eye and Golden or Yellow Apatite support your personal will, sense of authenticity and self-trust, and your ability to see the "bigger picture." Tiger's Eye works well if held to the forehead, between the eyes. Imagine you are seeing through the stone with this new Third Eye, and ask it to show you the truth about yourself. Really try to see things through this Third Eye stone as if you are moving your gaze up and to the center. Be a brave and bold Leo as you ask to see the truth and nothing but the truth.

Sunstone is feldspar with flashes of iridescent orange like sunlight. This stone can offer a sort of break from reality to reconnect with your *Self* and your individual moral or ethical code. As Leo is the holder of traditions and family values, Leo energy operates from a clear code of ethics and a strong sense of what is right and wrong. Tapping into this energy can help you transmute personal guilt into a state of personal justice. Use Sunstone to draw out Leo's sense of moral obligation and utilize that energy to take a bold action toward your goals.

Citrine always has a sunny disposition, much like the charming and charismatic Lion of the star chart. This stone clears "negativity" from all the chakra points and has a warm, solar connection. Similarly, Gold, while not a stone, is symbolically associated with the Sun and therefore with Leo energy. Use Gold as a metaphysical protection stone, like a spiritual shield providing a layer of protection between you and the energies that surround you, either as jewelry or in your hand. Nothing sticks to Gold, and it doesn't corrode, so it is a natural tool to draw upon when you need the courage and leadership qualities of the leonine star-energy.

VIRGO (AUGUST 23– SEPTEMBER 22)

Another human-shaped constellation, the Virgo star-pattern resembles a woman lounging on a chaise. This sign, like Gemini, is also ruled by the Roman God of Communication and the corresponding planet, Mercury.

Element: Earth

Chakras: Root, Heart, Throat, and Crown

Higher Path: Organized, methodical, clarity of thought and communication, and perfectionism

Lower Path: Critical, uptight, and anxious

Opposite sign: Pisces

Stones for Virgo: Cubic Fluorite, Pyrite, Optical Calcite, Sapphire, and any carved or cut gemstone

The perfectionistic, organized qualities of the Virgo energy are good for any manifestation of specific details. The stones that resonate with Virgo energy can help you to clear your mind and communicate directly and truthfully. These stones facilitate useful intentions when you embark on a new creative project that requires your focused attention to precise details. In their naturally occurring cubic shapes, Fluorite and Pyrite lend an organized energy to your environment and your activities there. Place a piece of Cubic Fluorite on your desk to keep your thoughts on track when you are at work on a computer or laptop. Place Fluorite or Pyrite in a plant pot near where you have to do detail-oriented work like paying bills, scheduling your family's transportation needs for the week, or making out a grocery list. This creates a kind of sympathetic circuit between the stone and the plant that can amplify that Virgo Earthy frequency. Just keep the plant close by, and don't forget to water and feed it.

Optical Calcite occurs in a cube, trapezoid, or rhombus-like shape and is clear as a water-streaked pane of glass. If you look carefully at Optical Calcite in the light, you may see a spray of semi-holographic rainbows within it. This stone is a spiritual magnifier and draws Virgoan qualities of clarity and precision to you when you need them. Select a piece of Optical Calcite which is as transparent as possible. Some stones come with various imperfections which may muddle the view. This is fine, but do seek out a piece of Optical Calcite through which you can see clearly. As you embark on detail-oriented work, literally *look through* this stone at the project at hand. Let it change your perspective a bit. Set the intention that this change of visual perspective will allow you to clarify and focus your work. Do this for several minutes. It may be helpful to keep a notebook and pen or other writing device nearby to collect your observations after this exercise. Reflect on this activity for a moment before moving back into your work.

With its beautiful blue hue, Sapphire resonates with perfection and purity as it calls up images of clear blue skies and calm tropical seas, or of the heavens of myth or religion. As one of the most valuable gemstones in the jewelry trade, it is easy, if not inexpensive, to find a piece of Sapphire jewelry to wear against the skin. You can also find raw or rough-cut Sapphires ranging from an opaque blue stone to a more transparent blue crystal. In rough form, these often resemble Lapis Lazuli (without the pyrite flecking or streaks) or Sodalite (without the white mottling).

Lastly, Virgo's organizational energy creates a tangible connection with any gemstone that has been cut into an organized symmetry regardless of color or type. These cut and polished stones exude the energy of Sacred Geometry, such as the star or tetrahedron, which symbolizes sacred connection between the light and shadow; the cube, which demonstrates divine balance; and the sphere, which resonates with the origins of life and creative energy. Additionally, cut stones have had a tremendous amount of energy fused into them by the jewelers who carved them. Just reflecting on the detail and precision that goes into carving a stone can help you draw up those Virgoan energies of organization and perfection.

LIBRA (SEPTEMBER 23– OCTOBER 22)

The Libra sign is a star cluster that resembles the Scales, or the measuring device that consists of two plates suspended from a kind of teeter-totter. This sign is also ruled by the Roman Goddess of Love and the planet named for her, Venus.

Element: Air

Chakras: Sacral, Heart, and Crown

Higher Path: Balanced partnerships, levelheadedness, conflict resolution or problem-solving, harmony, and justice

Lower Path: Self-sacrifice or martyrdom, confusion, and apathy or coldness

Opposite sign: Aries

Stones for Libra: Twin Point Quartz, Lepidolite, Flower Agate, Chrysocolla, Zeolite Formations, and Rose Quartz

Libra's energy is perhaps most strongly associated with balance and justice. This vibration aims to create both an inner sense of balance and stability and an external state of equilibrium which can either support or challenge external energies influencing your situation. This vibration will pull these energies closer to that central, neutral position. Libran energy can help you summon harmony, settle a dispute, resolve a conflict, or make a difficult decision which may be impacted by more than one domain (spiritual, emotional, intellectual, and so on). Stones which resonate with that balanced state work well to draw up this energy, or, in the alternative, placing stones *in a balanced state* can invoke those Libra senses. You might get a tabletop scale and place stones in both plates of the scale until you achieve a balanced central point. Another way to use stones to achieve balance is to place them on a tabletop or altar in a mandala-like pattern. Simply use your intuition to guide your placement of each stone into a balanced pattern. Reflect on the symmetry of the pattern you've created and ask yourself how you can pull that symmetry into the life situation where you wish to apply it.

Specific stones, such as a Twin Point or double-terminated Quartz Crystal, also amplify this vibration of balance and harmony. A Twin Point, sometimes called a Twin Quartz, has two similar points. Double-terminated refers to a Quartz wand which has two pointed ends. This stone is useful for decision-making with Libra energy. Start by drawing a mind map or simply listing out factors relating to a challenging choice you are facing. Branch out two different choices you may make and the likely costs and benefits (or pros and cons) of each choice. Now, holding your crystal in your hand, gaze softly at one point thinking about one side of the choice. See the choice play out like a movie on the crystal's surface. Repeat this activity with the other point. Jot down any clarity you received from crystal gazing. Now take three cleansing breaths and ask your inner Libra energy to come forth and make a choice.

Libran stones include Lepidolite and Flower Agate. Both calm anxiety and radiate an energetic field of ease for relaxed growth and development. Similarly, Chrysocolla can help you assert the Libran qualities of clear yet elegant personal boundaries infused with a sense of compassion straight from your Heart. Zeolites form in geometric formations along with other crystals and minerals, such as Calcite or Amethyst. Gazing at one while envisioning a healthy personal relationship can help you manifest a supportive partnership. Lastly, the versatile Rose Quartz attracts Libra's Venus-love qualities. It supports all things related to love and beauty, including healing your inner child so you can let go of any trauma you may have experienced in your young life to make way for you to experience love presently.

SCORPIO (OCTOBER 23– NOVEMBER 21)

This constellation resembles the Scorpion, and it is ruled by the Roman God of Death and the Underworld, Pluto, whose planetary counterpart was formerly believed to be a planet but is now known to be a dwarf planet thanks to our powerful, modern-age telescopes.

Element: Water

Chakras: Root, Sacral, and Third Eye

Higher Path: Transformation, leadership, and mastering the Shadow

Lower Path: Secrecy, cruelty, spitefulness, and depression

Opposite sign: Taurus

Stones for Scorpio: Selenite, Turquoise, Dioptase, Chiastolite, Black Calcite, Black Kyanite, and Lodolite

The Scorpio energy is one of transformation, and all of the stones associated with this sign carry similar watery, emotionally transformative vibrations. As a water sign, Scorpio resonates with all manner of emotion and emotional acceptance. Stones which resemble water or contain water (like Opal) work well for Scorpio vibrations, particularly those that are also associated with the ever-changing Moon, such as the lunar crystal Selenite. Because Scorpio is ruled by the planet Pluto, this vibration also invokes an experience of liminality, or the crossing of thresholds, such as those between major life events or sleeping and waking.

A Selenite wand can draw on the Scorpio energy of subconscious development. The wand shape of this form of crystallized gypsum targets your intentions. Point a Selenite wand literally at an object or symbol that you would like to personally transform. Maybe you want to channel grief at the passing of a loved one by pointing the wand at the obituary, or perhaps you may benefit from pointing the wand at the job listings on your local employment board. Use Selenite either to direct creative energy in or to draw energy out. Remember to set your intentions!

Turquoise and Dioptase are both very supportive of reorganizing areas of life. Take a piece of Turquoise to a nearby river or stream, or, if you don't live near moving water, you can run your faucet into a bowl in your sink. Hold the stone in the moving water for a few moments as you draw in a cleansing breath. Ask the water to help you change the things you imagined to be solid, whether those are limiting self-beliefs or relationships that you need to uncouple. When finished, pull the stone out and let it air dry in your hands as you imagine clearly how you will feel after the transformation. Repeat this activity for a week or until the change feels resolved. If you chose to perform this activity in your sink, please reuse the water, perhaps to nourish a house plant.

The Jungian Shadow is the part of your underlying personality which includes the things you may not like about yourself—the dark side. Scorpio is connected to that dark side as well as with the power of personal transformation necessary for you to embrace your whole self, Shadow and all. Some might describe the Shadow as the "bad" or "weak" qualities of your personality, but remember what we said about labeling things as negative. To transform yourself, you must first weave your Shadow into the Light by embracing it and letting it resonate with authenticity. As Scorpio is a Shadow work sign, stones associated with the Shadow, such as Black Calcite, Black Kyanite, and Lodolite (also known as Garden Quartz) can emphasize Scorpio energy. Ask your Shadow stones to present you with the parts of your *Self* you may be repressing and for the energy to accept these qualities.

SAGITTARIUS (NOVEMBER 22– DECEMBER 21)

The Archer Centaur constellation of Sagittarius resembles the half-man, half-horse creatures of myth. This planet is ruled by the Roman King of Gods and Justice-maker, the planet Jupiter.

Element: Fire

Chakras: Root, Sacral, Solar, and Throat

Higher Path: Personal truth, embodiment of ideals, and exploration

Lower Path: Abandonment, harsh communication, and escapism

Opposite sign: Gemini

Stones for Sagittarius: Pocket Stones, Picture Jasper, Geodes, Stalactite cuts, Fossils, and Merkaba Carved Stones

Sagittarius energy resonates with the concepts of Personal Journey and Truth. Because it is an authentic energy, it is good to wrap around any task which requires you to be vulnerable with others. Pocket stones and the stones that call you to pick them up when you are hiking or strolling along the beach typically resonate with the Sagittarian energy of journeys and personal experience because these stones themselves have experienced an authentic journey. To find your very own pocket stone, head out for a walk anywhere you may encounter a stone—even if it is gravel along a paved path near your house—or use a stone you purchased at a store. Before you pick up a stone in nature, please make sure you are legally allowed to do so, as many national parks forbid the removal of anything. As you walk or shop, silence your mind by focusing on your breath. If you catch your mind beginning to wander, just refocus your thoughts on your breath. Pay attention to the rhythm. When you are ready, look for a stone and select the first one that captivates you. Buy it or pick it up and place it in your pocket. This stone is now on the journey with you. Remind it (and remind yourself when you hold it) that you are on the right path.

Picture Jasper is commonly marked in patterns which resemble a Rorschach-style inkblot or a scenic etching. The veins and flecks in Picture Jasper often resemble a mountain or forest scene. They are fabulous for helping you picture yourself in the "right" place in your life. Geodes are like their own little worlds. This supports the Sagittarian theme of journeys and travel to new places. Stalactite cuts of gemstone and mineral often resemble an eye or a pair of eyes, as do many types of fossils. Since the subconscious works in symbolic language, this imagery connects your intuitive mind and inner truth to your outer experience by creating a kind of visual and tangible anchor. Merkaba is a sacred shape composed of two tetrahedrons or triangular pyramids. Both ancient and modern esoteric studies describe the Merkaba shape as an energetic vehicle which surrounds the physical and etheric body to support travel. Stones cut into these shapes are useful for this type of metaphorical journey.

CAPRICORN (DECEMBER 22– JANUARY 20)

This star constellation resembles the less well-known mythological character which is half-goat, half-fish, or the Goat Mermaid. Capricorn's energy is ruled by the Roman God of Agriculture and Time, the planet Saturn.

Element: Earth

Chakras: Root, Solar, Third Eye, and Crown

Higher Path: Achievement of goals, dedication, and material mastery

Lower Path: Material obsession, disconnection, and limitation

Opposite sign: Cancer

Stones for Capricorn: Lodestone, Magnetic Hematite, Malachite, Nuummite, Fluorite, and Shiva Lingam stones

Capricorn is an Earth sign which vibrates with tangibility and the energy of creation. This makes it an ideal energy to align you to the values you wish to manifest in your life, particularly anything on the physical plane (meaning things you might like to build or make with your hands). As Capricorn is governed by Saturn, or the divine personification of the sense of time and seasons, it can also be good to use Capricorn stones when you have something you need to endure over time.

Lodestone, a naturally occurring magnet which is typically found growing on another mineral or gemstone, or Magnetized Hematite will assist with manifesting the completion of projects. Because these stones literally attract other stones to them (or rather, metals), the Capricorn crystal intentions of goal achievement can draw your desire to you, magnetically aligning with your goals and experiences. Activate this energy by setting an intention into a Lodestone, and then write down a goal statement on a slip of paper. Use the Lodestone to stick the goal to your fridge and revisit it often.

Malachite has a high copper content and amplifies the will. Nuummite, a volcanic stone, is a deep black color with little flashes of gold, and it supports your manifestation. Just as thoughts and ideas are birthed from the "darkness" of the mental void, Nuummite is a dark stone that, itself, is metaphorically birthed from a volcano. Fluorite supports order for the material protocols necessary to create in the realm of tangible, physical things, and it can emphasize the Capricornian energy of material mastery. Shiva Lingam, a stone corresponding with the Capricorn-Earth qualities of stability and grounding, works almost like a battery, energizing your practice while keeping you rooted in the moment. The Shiva Lingam can ground your intentions to virtually any outcome or fulfillment.

AQUARIUS (JANUARY 21– FEBRUARY 18)

Aquarius is the star constellation that resembles a person carrying an amphora of water known as the Water Bearer. This sign is governed by Uranus, the obscure Roman God of the sky and planets.

Element: Air

Chakras: Throat, Third Eye, and Crown

Higher Path: Community, new thought, and greater good

Lower Path: Spacy, undisciplined, dismissive, and may have trouble manifesting in reality

Opposite sign: Leo

Stones for Aquarius: Aura-Treated Quartz, pieces with Rainbow Flashes, Scolecite, Faden Quartz, and Bismuth

The Aquarius energy is a fun-loving energy which thrives in social environments where friends can be made and sustained. This vibration is great for new relationships or community-level endeavors. This energy often exudes easy extroversion, but only when it comes to friends and friendships. The risk-taking (within reason) energy of the Aquarius vibration means finding a stone that truly resonates with your intentions to manifest your highest good is even more important.

Aura-Treated Quartz is essentially a natural Quartz stone which has been chemically bonded with various metals, creating an iridescent, multifaceted, colorful eye-catcher. This stone is technically manufactured, as it does not occur in nature in a raw form but must be factory created. Eye-drawing stones like Aura-Treated Quartz attract that Aquarian vibration of attention and recognition. Place a piece of this dazzling crystal in your workspace where others can see it. Let it travel with you and attract attention just as you yourself wish to attract the gaze of those around you. Aquarius' energy thrives in these higher realms and chakras, allowing the plays of color and unique shapes of the Aura-Treated Quartz to inspire or even communicate with you in unexpected ways.

Embracing the unexpected is the heart of the Aquarian energy— the *new* thought or direction. In the same vein as the Aura-Treated Quartz, really any stone that contains a flash or rainbow, such as Faden Quartz or the industrially refined metallic element Bismuth, can support the Aquarian energy of taking a new path or creating a new perspective. Use these sparkling stones to energize your exposure to new experiences. To keep yourself grounded during your exploration, simultaneously open the pathways of communication within yourself. Scolecite can assist with communication in the higher realms associated with Aquarian energy, such as the Spirit, the Higher Self, spirit guides, and Archangels.

PISCES (FEBRUARY 19–MARCH 19)

This constellation resembles a pair of fish forming a circle with their bodies. It is ruled by the Roman God of Transportation and the Sea, and by the planet named for that deity, Neptune.

Element: Water

Chakras: Sacral, Third Eye, and Crown

Higher Path: Spiritual development, intuition, and completion

Lower Path: Extreme sensitivity, lethargy, and dependence

Opposite sign: Virgo

Stones for Pisces: Iolite, Elestial Quartz, Ocean Jasper, Crystal Ball, Seer Stones, and Howlite

While it is typical of Water sign energy to be strongly associated with emotions and emotional stability, Pisces is perhaps the poster child for this quality. When you wish to project or experience a truly compassionate, loving energy, then Piscean stones can generate that vibration. Similarly, spirituality is often said to develop with perfect love and trust in yourself (or self-compassion), so you can connect deeply to your spirituality by invoking stones with the energy of Pisces.

Iolite was once used by the Vikings as part of the compass navigational system that helped their people traverse uncharted waters far from home. Iolite's connection to the sea, and therefore to the Piscean energy of Neptune and travel, is worth noting as a resource to expand self-awareness and internal navigation. Ocean Jasper is gentle and supportive. It can help you surrender to the flow and relax into the current of the Universe as opposed to fighting against it. Howlite is a similarly relaxing stone that is so intensely calming it has been known to induce sleep during healing sessions.

Two additional types of Pisces-vibe stones can enhance clairvoyance and clairsentience when scrying or gazing at light reflected in the surface of them: Crystal Balls and Seer Stones. To scry, be sure to select a smooth, clear stone and give it a quick polish with a soft cloth first. Set it near a sunny window or next to a flickering light such as a candle flame, so that the image of shadow and light reflected on its surface is not static but dynamic. Some choose to add smoke from a smudge stick, like white sage, and fan the smoke over the stone's surface with a feather. As you gaze into the polished sheen, soften your gaze and ask to see inside yourself to what you really want or think. Allow the images to come to you without judgment. This is your intuition speaking to you through images you knit together from the light playing on the surface of these stones. Listen to yourself. What are you saying?

CHAPTER 10

STONES, CRYSTALS, AND ORGANICS: A PRIMER OF SHAPES AND TYPES

While we tend to use the terms "gemstones," "stones," and "crystals" interchangeably, there are actually categorical differences between the different types of minerals and stones we use in our energy and relaxation work. These may be useful to know as you determine the types of relaxation and energy healing you may do.

For example, Coral, Pearl, Jet, and Amber are not stones but organic materials which have been either petrified or fossilized, as with Jet and Amber, or harvested by farming or killing living creatures, as with Coral or Pearl. We also include distinctly shaped stones and crystals that can amplify our wellness activities. And, of course, any stone can be faked with resin and plastic casting or with chemical engineering. Many people who feel drawn to crystals often discover that part of the attraction is the fact that real crystals and stones have spent millions of years growing in the Earth and are therefore deeply connected with nature. It's hard to get that same vibration from a Quartz Crystal you discover is actually made from resin poured into a mold.

SHAPES AND VARIETIES OF STONES, CRYSTALS, MINERALS, AND ORGANICS

Stones and crystals have a long history of dazzling people with their unusual characteristics. When you consider that Quartz Crystal makes up almost 12 percent of the Earth's crust and only forms into its hard, geometric, crystalline form over millions of years and with lots of pressure and sometimes heat, it makes sense that people would be fascinated by these sparkling elements. Digging them up, offering them on altars, shaping them into jewelry, adorning ourselves with them, and giving them to one another as tokens of affection all point to the rich connection people have with these Earthy energies.

What might be even more fascinating is the fact that people have been amplifying the energy of crystals for thousands (maybe even tens of thousands) of years before we had the technology necessary to show us their unique qualities. Crystals specifically are marvelous expressions of order out of chaos. Under a high-powered microscope, the crystal shape is a series of perfectly ordered lattices of molecules, forming a kind of structured net held together by the same energy that holds together all matter in the Universe. When you think about it, then, these shiny bits of geometry poking out of the Earth's surface are more organized than even our best computer programs.

It is little wonder why crystals have been used for millennia to focus and amplify energy—whether the energy of human intention and thought or the energy of mechanisms like clocks and lasers. It turns out that the unique and tightly organized lattices that have made crystals so visually appealing to people throughout history also offer a stable structure for the movement of electrical energy and are highly coveted for their use in electronics as a result. Could the early civilizations which capped their spiritual towers with crystals and stones and made giant effigies to their deities out of Citrine or Amethyst have known that crystals were such powerful conductors?

Many of the materials, however, that we include as previously noted under the label of "gemstone" are neither crystalline nor stone. Not every stone comes out of the Earth in a hexagonal prism or cluster or points, nor does every stone come as hard as diamonds. Some stones are so fragile they will dissolve in water or can break off into shards or splinters that can become lodged under the skin. Even more importantly, some stones we consider beautiful to behold or that

serve excellent energy healing purposes are actually toxic and slough
off a layer of dust that can be extremely harmful—or even deadly,
under the right circumstances—if ingested. As you work with stones
and crystals, you will start to evolve your instincts about how to use
them. In some cases, you will hold crystals or lay them on your body.
Some crystals you may even place into water to infuse their energy
healing elements into something you can spray on other objects, but
not all stones are created equal. Basic crystal and stone care should
help you make safe choices about what stones to use and in what
contexts so you don't get poisoned, splintered and jabbed by shards,
accidentally dissolve your great grandmother's natural pearl necklace
in the glass of water you were using to clean it up, or wake up from
an afternoon nap to discover your Rose Quartz has gone from pink to
clear in color! We'd hate for you to drop a rock into a vessel of water
to cleanse it overnight under moonlight only to discover that it has
dissolved, and we'd especially hate to learn that you drank from water
that had a poisonous crystal in it!

Basic Types and Shapes of Stones

Stone and Rock: Stone typically refers to gems and minerals that
can be found inside of rocks, which can come in any shape or size
and often contain different gems, minerals, and metals within them.
In the simplest sense, rock is the product of molten lava that has
cooled over billions of years and floated to the surface of water.
Various rocks, such as Granite, contain many different minerals
inside them. Granite, for example, often contains flecks of shiny
mica and Quartz Crystal. Unlike the minerals we think of as crystals,
stones tend to form amorphously—that is, they may have crystalline
qualities but don't *look* like the geometric crystals we think of when we
imagine them.

Crystal: Crystals are minerals that form when the molecules that make them up—often the same molecules that make up stones—combine in a lattice formation, like a net that extends in all directions. Crystals seem to "grow" out of rock formations or inside of them, as with geodes. Because crystals are structural, they can also be grown or engineered in labs or created using chemicals. Since most naturally occurring crystals take millions of years of pressure, heating, and weathering to form, they tend to be stronger and harder than their chemical mimics.

Organic Material: Certain so-called gemstones are not actually stones at all, but organic material. Jet, for instance, sometimes called the "witch's stone," is a form of lignite that looks very much like coal and is derived from decayed wood. Amber is actually fossilized tree sap, and it can come in many different colors from green to red to orange. Coral is a sea creature, an invertebrate that can only live while under seawater in its unique environment; the vast amount of Coral you can purchase in the marketplace is actually the skeletal remains of once-living sea creatures. Pearls, both fresh and saltwater, form inside a mollusk when an irritant like a grain of sand works its way into the mollusk's shell; as a defense mechanism, the creature coats it with successive layers of fluid, and the particle eventually becomes a pearl. A naturally occurring pearl can only be discovered when a mollusk is forced open, thus killing it. There are other examples of organic matter we lump into the category of stone, such as the fossils of ammonites or clams, but those mentioned above are the most common materials you will encounter on the gem market.

 Tumbled Stones: A tumbled stone has been polished with grit to produce a smooth surface with a sheen. Some tumbled stones, like Labradorite and Opal, reveal an iridescent sparkle or "flash" that is highly valued by energy workers and healers. Tumbled stones come in all shapes and sizes.

Palm Stones: A palm stone is a variety of tumbled stone that fits comfortably in the palm of your hand, usually held in place against the palm by the muscles of the thumb, index, and little fingers. Because of the natural fit a palm stone has to a person's hand, palm stones are excellent for relaxation, particularly when used by practitioners who perform relaxation therapies on clients, as you can use your hand to direct where you wish the energy to go.

Wand or Natural Point: Wands and natural points are crystals that are typically pointed on one end and flat or rough on the other end, or *single-terminated*. It is possible to have a *double-terminated* wand in which both ends of the shaft come to a point, though these occur naturally much less frequently. Natural points, as the name implies, occur in nature as crystals "grow" outward into this pointed, wand-like shape. Wands are great for pointed or targeted energy work.

Twin Point: Sometimes called "soul" points, a crystal twin occurs when two points come out on the same side of a shaft, like twins standing side by side.

Abundance: These crystals are similar to *clusters* in that there are several crystal points clustered together at the base, but a single point rises higher than the rest.

Phantoms: Ghost or phantom-like, crystals sometimes grow inside other crystals. When this happens, they are called phantoms as you can often see through the translucent outer crystal to the ghost-like crystal growing in its middle.

Generator: Generators tend to be six-sided, singular pointed crystals that are short and fat. They can occur naturally, but many on the market are fabricated through cutting, tooling, or even simulation with resins and plastics.

Geode: A Geode is a hollowed-out rock that contains crystal formations within it. Geode-hunters have to become very good at recognizing the pocked exteriors of naturally occurring geodes, because, to most of us, they just look like big, gray rocks. Crack them open, though, and discover a glittering world inside!

Clusters: These are multiple crystal points that come out from a mass of mineral. They may not have a single outcropping and may appear to be more chaotic than abundance crystal formations or clearly terminated crystal rods.

Sphere: These do not occur naturally, though some crystals, such as Grape Agates, do form in orbs. A sphere or "crystal ball" is shaped from a larger piece of crystal by tooling and cutting it into a ball-like shape.

Pyramid: Pyramid-shaped crystals have four rather than six sides terminating to a point. These do occasionally show up naturally with certain minerals, but most of the pyramids you will find are artificially shaped.

Square: Square or cubic crystals do occur naturally, or else they can be cut into shape. Many Calcite and Fluorite cubes may have been harvested in natural formations.

Occluded: Occlusions are the presence of other minerals or metals appearing along the outside or even within another crystal and are typically seen as a slight veil or iridescence.

Inclusion: Similar to Occlusions, however, these appear more dense or solid and are visible within the primary stone, such as in Lodolite or Tourmaline Inclusion Quartz.

Other Shapes: There are dozens of other shapes that occur naturally and artificially in crystals and stones. Gem cutters will occasionally shape natural stones simply to bring out their luster. Stones that have a naturally occurring hole in the center are sometimes called fairy stones, for instance. Eggs, which are generally shaped by gem-workers, are said to represent the cosmic creation myth (the snake and bird eggs). And shards or splinters of gypsum (Selenite) or Kyanite and other soft crystals are more like "chips" of a rock and may have many different shapes.

FIFTY CRYSTALS, STONES, AND ORGANICS (ALPHABETICAL)

Agate: This is a very versatile stone that comes in many different colors, some of which have intricate patterns that resemble lace, the rings of a tree trunk, or even mossy or fern-like landscapes. For this reason, Agate can really be pulled into representing any of the chakras or the four elements (Earth, Air, Fire, and Water) because it has colors and patterns that draw out the characteristics of each element. When used in energy healing work, Agate is excellent for tasks related to balancing the shakti (yin) and shiva (yang) energies of the Kundalini pathway along the spine. This stone naturally comes in every color of the rainbow; however, it is one that is commonly dyed to more saturated tones of blue, pink, and purple. Bands of color or pocked, mossy droplets that may occur naturally characterize this stone as a lively landscape for relaxation work.

Agate's vibe is in our experience supportive and nurturing, which makes it a great stone for relaxation, relieving stress, and calming energy. It can be a very useful stone to use to teach children about their feelings and empower them with supportive tools.

Amber: While actually the petrified or fossilized sap of a tree rather than a stone, this hardened plant resin is used by healers to connect with Earth energy, solidity, the Root, and abundance. Generally, Amber will come in shades of orange to brown, though there are some varieties of green and milky Amber. Amber can contain other organic matter, such as insects, and these are often coveted for their multiple energies and the power of both the Amber and the creature or element within. This organic material is invigorating to both the mind and body. It is said to warm when worn on the skin, and it is a soft enough material that it is possible to accidentally dissolve it in water. Due to its natural, orangey color, Amber is best used on the Sacral Chakra to open your senses of security, abundance, and pleasure. Amber bead necklaces have been used by some healers to diminish teething pain in infants, though they can pose a choking hazard. Amber is strongest when received as a gift. Once you have used up the energy your Amber has to offer you, cleanse it and then pass it along to a new caretaker to "restart" its juju.

Amber is an excellent go-to when seeking support and resources, as it resembles the golden elixir of Mother Earth. Hold it in your hands and focus on connecting to the ever-present Earth energies, which are richly abundant and available to us all. Visualize a golden current channeled up through your feet, legs, and Root Chakra.

Amethyst: A form of silicon dioxide like most crystals (including all quartz varieties, citrine, opal, jasper, chrysoprase, and chalcedony, to name a few), Amethyst is a common stone bearing tremendous value to healers. In fact, if you acquire only a few stones, make sure one is an Amethyst cluster. Much of the Amethyst on the market is dyed Quartz Crystal. True Amethyst will fade if left in the sunlight, and, if you let it get covered with dust, you may never see its purple luster again. When heated naturally in the Earth, Amethyst turns honey-colored and transforms into Citrine. Amethyst is heavily associated with the mind, so it's no wonder that it is often used in Crown Chakra work for ascension, connection with our energy bodies, or trance work to enhance sleep and lucid dreaming. Wearing Amethyst is particularly lucky, and we advise either setting it in natural fiber (such as hemp or cotton macramé) or in sterling silver. Wear it bound to a headband or barrette for Crown Chakra work, or over the heart to help circulate that energy from heart to head and back again. Amethyst is also an excellent crystal for working with grief and the loss of a loved one.

Amethyst would be a stone we would suggest when you wish to connect to more Spiritual or Mystic aspects of life. Should you wish to use Amethyst to support lucid dreaming, we would suggest you pair it with a Brecciate Jasper and a Howlite to counterbalance any "buzzy" effect from the Amethyst and to support dream recall.

Aquamarine: This stone is actually a Beryl, just like Emerald, and typically comes in a seafoam blue or green color, though some slivers of this stone are so translucent they appear clear with a light blue sheen. A strong connection with the ocean makes this stone an excellent travel-stone. If you are away from home, Aquamarine can help you draw the security of home to you from across the waves on the wind. This crystal works best in the Throat Chakra and can aid with communication by infusing us with the courage to speak up and out. Many people choose Aquamarine to refine intuition. Particularly worn as jewelry set in sterling silver, Aquamarine is a great intention stone for manifesting the secrets of our souls that are perhaps veiled even from ourselves.

Because Aquamarine is such a peaceful stone and forms in six-sided, hexagonal shapes, we suggest working with it to promote visions of peace on Earth. To do this, cultivate a sense of peace within yourself and intentionally bring that vibration into the Earth realm by virtue of your vibrational presence and resonance with this gentle stone.

Aventurine: Most Aventurine on the market is green, but there are lesser known varieties of this stone which come in peach, orange, red, blue, and golden. Depending on the color, its use may vary. Green Aventurine crystal intentions are helpful for manifesting financial abundance, opening the heart, and comforting you in your darkest moments. Green aventurine is also useful for relaxing forms of self-love and self-protection. Meditating on this stone can help you to feel safe, energized, and hopeful.

Green Aventurine is an excellent choice to work with during Mercury Retrogrades, times known for disruptions in communication as well as technological issues. Because Mercury is the closest planet to the Sun, it can appear to move backward in the sky, and this accounts for the term "retrograde." This occurs several times in a year and can cause you to feel unable to communicate or accomplish tasks. To counteract this phenomenon, simply wear a piece of Green Aventurine in jewelry or place it in your pocket with the intention for it to support you during this somewhat challenging time.

Bloodstone: Bloodstone, like Quartz Crystal, is silicon dioxide and is characterized by its veins of iron that deposit blood-red pockets and arteries of rusty iron in this stone. This stone has also been called Heliotrope, which is the name of a flower as well. Some legends suggest that anointing a bloodstone with the dew of a morning Heliotrope can turn the sun red in the sky.[13] Perhaps owing to its iron-bearing qualities, bloodstone is great for purifying the blood and reducing anemia in those who wear it. Bloodstone crystal intentions are good to help you focus on the immune system and its health, stability, and fortitude. One of us recalls the bloodstone used on the body, moving around the neck, in a specific effort to ward off what some might call "psychic vampire attacks" and what others might call simply the draining complainer in your environment dragging everyone down. Bloodstone, in these cases, is a great anchor to the self; with its support, you don't slosh around in the quicksand of those well-meaning souls whose woes can be contagiously stressful to empaths. Energy healers and relaxation specialists who plan to use this stone to work with others should consider carrying a piece on their person to help improve the ability to be a supportive energy in a person's life without losing oneself to that person's need.

Bloodstone is an excellent choice when you are looking to connect with the past for the purpose of healing. For example, if you have a past trauma or a difficult memory you wish to process, you may use this stone to meditate and send the energy of forgiveness, gratitude, or abundance to your past self or your family members in the past. You might picture a strand of DNA or imagine your family tree and mentally move along that astral thread back in time to the point you wish to heal.

---

13   We recommend Gemlore for further study on this crystal's features.

Calcite: This stone is sometimes easily mistaken for Quartz Crystal as some varieties grow in clear clusters. Its rhomboidal shape suggests to the undiscerning eye that it might be a double-pointed Quartz Crystal. From an energetic viewpoint, Calcite also bears similarities to Quartz in that it is an excellent amplifier of energy and can run like a battery, charging up the energy of all the other crystals and objects around it. While Clear Calcite is coveted for manifestation rituals, cuboidal "Optical Calcite" is used for the creation of "windows," as Optical Calcites are cubes of Clear Calcite that are transparent enough to read words *through* it like glass. Optical Calcite often has many stunning holographic looking rainbows visible within, and it is sometimes called Rainbow Calcite or Hologram Calcite. Calcite actually comes in many different varieties and is commonly found in American geodes and Zeolite. Calcite commonalities come in clear, blue, orange, yellow, green, red, pink, and less often black, making it a crystal that can be used for virtually any work on the energy chakras or meridians. In its water-clear form, the material can be polished into a transparent cube or rhombus. Peering through such a clear stone at the world around you can impart a sense of clarity about the world within you. For that reason, Clear Optical Calcite can help you clarify your intentions. Relax with Calcite by infusing that clear slice of crystal with an intention to see and show the truth. You can also use it to create a picture block dedicated to an ancestor to infuse your belated relative with a clear path to love. Just place the Calcite cube in front of a photograph on a shelf to peer through it. Of course, Calcite comes in other colors which are less translucent. Pink Calcite, for instance, triggers similar outcomes as Rose Quartz does to foster a loving, safe place, which is the *cornerstone* of relaxation.

As Calcite comes in so many colors and is incredibly energizing, it is an excellent stone to boost the energy of a corresponding chakra point. As Black Calcite is a little harder to find, particularly in smaller pieces, in our experience, when one crosses your path, it may be a sign that a period of shadow work is needed or approaching. The Shadow is a Jungian psychological perspective that parts of ourselves might be hard to accept or embrace, but it is your whole self, both sunshine and shadow, that must resonate in harmony to achieve authenticity. Shadow work is a time to reflect on ourselves as whole and to either heal or incorporate facets of our Divine being.

Carnelian: This ancient stone has a rich history, and it is referenced many times in ancient lapidaries, or "books written about the properties of stones and crystals." It comes in red, orange, pink, or brown, but the most coveted color is red. Carnelian reminds us of hot, red blood. In this way, it is easy to connect Carnelian through correspondence to the blood of life, menstruation, iron-rich blood, nourishment, and health, and all the strength and fortitude buttressing the Root Chakra. Even the orange versions of Carnelian tend to gravitate to the Root Chakra moreso than to the Sacral Chakra, but, of course, each stone is unique. According to Diane Morgan, author of *Gemlore: Ancient Secrets and Modern Myths from the Stone Age to the Rock Age,* "From very early times (at least 2000 BCE), Carnelian has been created by heating Chalcedony, and most Carnelian on the market today has been heat-treated. While fine natural Carnelian can be found, it's more economical by far to heat-treat lower grade material" (pg. 40),[14] which of course means that many of the Carnelian options you find on the market began as other stones. In its truest form, a silicon dioxide Chalcedony, Carnelian can be used to strengthen the bond between a parent and her child or to help you recover from the things that slow you down—everything from heartbreak to fatigue to procrastination. Carnelian is an excellent focusing stone for energizing relationships and action.[15]

14 We mention this book in several places because it is an excellent reference book for both the historical significance and an almost anthropological understanding of how people have used and interpreted the qualities of stones and crystals over thousands of years. Morgan, Diane. *Gemlore: Ancient Secrets and Modern Myths from the Stone Age to the Rock Age.* Westport, CT: Greenwood, 2008.

15 Gem healer and author Judy Hall describes Carnelian as a trust stone. The details around this stone can be found in her book The Crystal Bible: A Definitive Guide to Crystals. Cincinnati, OH: Walking Stick Press, 2003. We highly recommend this book for those looking for a quick-reference overview of stones (as it includes more than two hundred).

Carnelian is a stone that can connect you with your primal instinct. It can help you to get out of your head and into your body. Often logic overpowers instinct. You may feel the vibes of your intuition trying to communicate something to you, but your lower mind begins to paint the picture in another way. You may let your mind overpower your instincts in the moment and close yourself off to that intuitive vibration and then kick yourself later for not trusting your gut. Carnelian's energy can help you tap into that vibration, listen to your instincts, and trust your intuition.

Celestite / Celestine: While Celestite comes in yellow, red, and white, it's the blue variety that seems to have created its name, as it looks like a cluster of soft-twinkling, sky blue gems glittering in a white-cloud rock base. Celestite often looks its most attractive as a cluster for this very reason, but of course you can find celestite crystal points and wands as well. With a high vibration and frequency, this stone can be used to develop the Third Eye's connection to spiritual guides and Angels. Because it comes in a paler shade of blue, it can also be a useful Throat stone as a focal point for constructive, truthful dialogue. In fact, Celestite is coveted for its serene sky and cloud appeal because it seems to settle things peacefully and seek out truth. Celestite does have a small risk of fading if left in direct sunlight, and, in cluster form, the stone peaks can be accidentally chipped or crumbled out of its Geode shell. This stone resonates when placed on a shelf in front of a mirror so it can reflect its vibration.

Celestite has such a dreamy, soft, angelic vibration and packs a (surprising) little punch. We suggest this stone often for those beginning to study divination or other universal communication methods, such as sacred geometry or numerology.

Chalcedony: It seems to one of us (Araminta) that every geode she has ever cracked over the decades she has spent rockhounding over the stony, forest-studded mountainsides of Maine has been a

Chalcedony Geode. Of course, geodes are a little hard to find, but Chalcedony seems to be the most plentiful type. Like the Quartzes, Chalcedony is made up of silicon dioxide. It comes in white, blues and grays, and pinks and reds, and it can be difficult to identify a blue Chalcedony when it is side-by-side with a white one, as they can seem like entirely different stones. This geometry of stones within stones resonates with fertile energies and can help inspire creative processes.

Because we often find Chalcedony in geodes, the sacred stone eggs of the Universe, Chalcedony resonates with a maternal, nurturing energy and can therefore be used to clear a space of negativity. Setting cracked Chalcedony geodes in the four corners of your home can create an X-patterned energy flow that functions like an early warning system to clear and nurture the spaces you occupy.

Chrysocolla: This stone, which is often found in rich shades of deeply oceanic blue and green, is well known for its communication skills. Its mottled blue color comes from the oxidized copper contained in the substance of this stone. Perhaps owing to its vigorous blue sheen, Chrysocolla is a natural stone for the Throat Chakra and all things connected to communication or teaching. Known as both the "self-awareness stone" and the "communication stone," Chrysocolla is at its most magical and sacred when it is beside your bed to clear out bad thoughts and dreams.

Beautiful for bridging the Heart and Throat, Chrysocolla is ideal for heart-based communication and intentions and for approaching expression from the Soul. This stone can help you with the discomfort of confrontation, particularly when you need to confront someone you love with whom you need to gently set a healthy boundary. Chrysocolla supports effective, purposeful communication without sugarcoating or dismissing important issues.

Chrysoprase: A personal favorite of both the writers of this book, Chrysoprase is a beautiful, green, often black-veined stone that is beautifully aligned with the Heart Chakra and matters of love and other watery, flowy emotions. The black veining in Chrysoprase is composed of nickel, and often a chunk of raw Chrysoprase can be found embedded in a coarse black "rind," making it look a bit like a sea-green watermelon. Given the importance of the Heart Center in all matters of energy work, Chrysoprase is a critical addition to any energy healer's tool kit, as it is the stone of joy and optimism. A type of Beryl (like Emerald), it's a hard stone that comes in a variety of greens and greenish-blues. It is an excellent stone for overall wellness.

Chrysoprase supports patience with yourself and with others. It is therefore a top suggestion for cultivating forgiveness and grace. When you think of forgiveness, your mind may travel to an example of a person you feel wronged you in some way. Can you call up this example in your mind now? Chrysoprase can help you focus your forgiveness of that person and release the burden you carry. It also works acutely. Use this stone to resolve miscommunications and misunderstandings with your partner, frustration with other drivers in traffic, or impatience with yourself for forgetting an item on your shopping list. It is these little things that can sometimes spiral and ruin your day. Chrysoprase supports both long-term and short-term forgiveness of Self and others.

Cinnabar: This is one of the more toxic stones, and it should be handled with extreme caution as the dust that might rub off onto your hands while holding it will need to be immediately washed off to avoid accidental ingestion. Cinnabar is an ore of mercury (the stone is technically mercury sulfide, which means it also contains sulfur), so it is primarily mercury poisoning you should fear (the same madness that struck the Hatter in *Alice in Wonderland*). Cinnabar is appealing as a stone because it tends to grow as a matrix out of other crystal clusters, and so it often appears as a brilliantly colored scarlet or maroon against the other crystals where it may be growing. It is also a stone referenced often in alchemical texts from the Middle Ages, and therefore it can have a remarkable transformative effect on you.[16] Because Cinnabar is often mined from volcanoes, it is often associated with transformation and abrupt, needful, dramatic change.

Cinnabar is a very good relaxation stone if your crystal intention is to charge yourself for a major shift in your life path. As both a highly toxic stone and a stone associated with volcanoes, Cinnabar is best handled as a meditation stone. Place it on a clean surface or altar and align it with three red candles. Allow the candle flame to flicker on the stone while you gaze at it and count your breaths.

Citrine: The first time you find a Citrine cluster or tower, you may notice how much Citrine looks like an orange-dyed cluster of Amethyst—and you would not be far off the mark. Many pieces of Citrine on the market today are heat-treated Amethyst, a process which essentially burns the crystal into an orangey-yellow or singed crystal. As you might expect, Citrine is another silicon dioxide, making it a member of the family of silicates that includes the most organized crystal patterns and Quartzes. Golden Topaz, a similarly yellow stone, is often mistaken for natural Citrine. In its truest state, Citrine can connect the dots between the physical body and the subtle body. An almost honey golden yellow, the color of the Solar Plexus Chakra, Citrine resonates with the body and the five (or more) sensations within it. The organized structure of Citrine also resonates a mirror, subtle body, and it is a strong stone for connecting the senses with the energies (thoughts or emotions) through intention and manifestation of the waking, authentic self. There are few more effective ways to relax than by starting with the sensory body and energetically connecting those senses to the subtle body. Citrine is an excellent conduit for this type of deep and lasting relaxation.

---

16 Paracelsus, also known as Philippus Theophrastus Bombast, wrote of Cinnabar in his alchemical text *The Treasure of Treasures for Alchemists* sometime in the early sixteenth century. He cited this stone as one of the key ingredients in the alchemical pursuit of the Philosopher's Stone, or the pursuit of turning a base metal into gold.

True, natural Citrine has a warm and sunny energy which empowers the higher will as opposed to the will of the ego. This is a perfect stone for the crystal intention of healing the ego. Use this stone to direct your will and channel personal energy to your higher goals, projects, and desired fulfillments.

Coral: Coral is one of the organic substances we often include in our list of crystals and gemstones; however, Coral is actually the skeletal remains of once-living creatures that were killed to become decoration. It is no secret that the Coral reefs are presently facing unprecedented danger from over-harvesting and chemical runoff from things you might not even imagine—sunblock, for example, can contain damaging chemicals that decimate Coral colonies, killing off these creatures that are so very necessary to marine life. As such, the writers of this book humbly ask that you purchase no Coral from any distributor but rather seek it out from secondhand and thrift stores, where all the items for sale have been donated. This will offer you some assurance that no one is directly profiting from the Coral you purchase, as it's essentially a hand-me-down. And we likewise implore you not to harvest your own living Coral pieces, no matter how tempting. Many white sand beaches get their color from Coral, and you might get lucky and find a piece yourself while walking the shore.

If Coral is essential to your manifestation, energetic intention, or relaxation work, then we recommend you work with it while it is living—manifest an image of Coral in your mind while you submerge yourself in water near living Coral (using a reef-safe sunscreen), and commune with the living Coral's intricate web of life. Coral is essentially made of the mineral calcium carbonate, much like the Pearl but with a different chemical structure. According to Diane Morgan, in ancient alchemical texts which were focused on the process of transmuting one inferior substance into another superior substance, Coral is "materia prima, in that it is material not yet fixed by air." (pg. 58) Many ancient cultures equated Coral with the blood of Medusa. The same blood of myth that produced the legendary flying horse Pegasus when it dripped on the ground was said to have dripped into the sea, creating the first Coral reefs.[17] The symbolic representation of Medusa's blood can be invoked for protection as her face adorned the ancient images of the goddess Athena's shield for that very reason.

Relaxing with ethical Coral in your palms or pressed to your heart, throat, or forehead might help you get past an obstacle and transform your energy from inertia to movement once again.

Diamond: You'd be hard-pressed to find a person who has not heard at least a dozen stories of the hardest stone substance as yet known on the planet; Diamonds are used to express the tenderest of love between two people at the point of engagement, and they are also used in ultra-diverse laser tools for intricate surgeries. Diamonds are arguably the hardest mineral on Earth, yet they tend to get lumped into the same category as Rubies, Sapphires, and Emeralds even though they have no real shared structure. Diamonds are made up of carbon and register a hardness of ten on the Mohs' scale. This hardness scale is used to determine practical things like what kind of tools you will need to cut or polish a stone, and with Diamond pretty much only other diamonds can really help shape this valuable stone. To give you an idea of the respective hardness, then, an Emerald is just a 7.5 on that scale as compared to a diamond's rating of ten, and both types of corundum (Sapphire and Ruby) have a hardness of nine. Diamonds are a thousand times harder than Quartz crystals, and they are easily the most expensive gemstone or crystal on the

---

17   Medusa is of special interest to one of the writers of this book, Araminta Star Matthews, who sees the tale of this often-misunderstood mythological woman as a sacred narrative reflecting the story of how our greatest weaknesses can also be our greatest strengths. The idea that Coral is connected to such a mythology as the gazing Gorgon with her stony eyes might even imply that Coral is the remnants of the first creatures turned to stone by the Medusa gaze. For more information about Coral, check out Diane Morgan's *Gemlore: Ancient Secrets and Modern Myths from the Stone Age to the Rock Age.* Westport, CT: Greenwood, 2008.

market (but, ironically, they are not the most scarce—Rubies have that honor).

Diamonds are not likely to be found in your local crystal shop, and, most often, they are paired with metals in jewelry. As there is a terrible backstory of human trafficking being used to secure slave labor to mine Diamonds, we encourage you to seek ethical sources and to investigate the origins of the stone you are purchasing.

Diamonds have a clarity and density that evoke a very high vibrational frequency. Work with Diamonds to connect to the higher realms. Diamond earrings may be worn with intention to hear signs and signals which will trigger you to pay attention during life-altering moments or when choices arise that may support your highest vibration. This may come with a sensation like a ringing in the ears.

Emerald: Though often categorized as being in the same mineral family as Diamonds, Rubies, and Sapphires, the Emerald is actually a bit of a black sheep in that it is a Beryl. Both Sapphires and Rubies are a form of corundum made up of alumina and oxygen, making them only marginally less hard according to Mohs' Hardness scale than Diamonds, which are carbon. Emeralds are also major energy amplifiers, so tune into the vibrational climate in order to use them to your advantage. If you anticipate you will have a stressful day, you might choose to avoid Emerald in order to contain that vibrational energy and prevent amplification of the stress. Alternatively, if you plan to spend the day with a loved one or taking a restorative yoga class, carry Emerald to enhance those pleasant vibes.

Use Emeralds when you want to create an anchor to a memory or feeling in order to more easily cultivate this feeling again when manifesting. For example, when you are authentically tapping into the feeling of gratitude, love, or prosperity, sit with Emerald and allow this vibration to wash over you and into the stone. Next time you want to manifest that feeling, use the Emerald in your ritual or meditations.

Fluorite: This calcium fluoride crystal often includes a rainbow within it like the glittering iris of the eye. The rainbow variety of Fluorite often has blue, green, yellow, and violet layers in the center of a clear crystalline point or generator. It is mostly the rainbow within this stone that gives it its symbolic purpose. Fluorite unifies the chakras and particularly resonates with the Heart, Throat, Third Eye, and Crown to draw your energy upward and into your spirit. Yellow varieties of Fluorite resonate with the Solar Plexus and Sacral energy circles. We recommend placing a Fluorite tower or sphere on your desk near any electronic devices you might be using (including your phone) to steady your energy and ensure the vibrations of your work don't interfere with the vibrations of your body; to put it more directly, Fluorite can help you refocus your energy away from technical work and back into your body so you can set aside the constant crush and whir of electronic attentions.

Fluorite supports clarity, seeing the whole picture, and connecting with your inner truth. When you are resolving any problem, use Fluorite to set intentions for clarity and order during meditation. Ask the stone to clarify the messages you receive. Listen carefully to your inner voice, and then write down what you heard in a notebook. What did you learn about yourself and your inner thoughts?

Garnet: When cut, polished, and set in a ring, this stone is often mistaken for its much harder red stone sister, Ruby. Garnets tend to grow in clusters that cause them to look like the red, pulpy seeds of the pomegranate, which is a symbol connected to the ovary, full of seeds of new life, and to the afterlife. In the Greek myth of Persephone, we learn of a young woman who is bound to the underworld because she was persuaded to eat a few of these pomegranate seeds, forever linking death and fertility in the symbolic

mind. Garnet was even said to have illuminated Noah's ark.[18] There
are many varieties of Garnet ranging in color from black, brown, and
red to green and even yellow. Perhaps because of their rich blood-
red color, red Garnets are great stones for connecting with the Root
Chakra. With Garnet in hand, you can connect with your abundant
blood, and, if you pay careful enough attention, you can both hear
and feel that blood pulsing through your veins and arteries. This
stone's connection to life-changing transitions also makes it a powerful
stone for manifesting ease while going through these changes,
including finding peace during the exultation of childbirth or finding
solace during the grief of loss due to death.

*Garnet is sold in many forms, including chunky, rounded, and meteoric shapes and
carved cabochons. Connect the physical with the visual when attuning to Garnet,
and use its shape to assist you. A meteoroid-shaped stone might inspire impact,
while a flat or cabochon piece may feel more like a shield or a solar panel colleting
Pranic energy and directing it to your own vital force.*

Hematite: The root word for "blood" (*haima* in middle English)
is part of this stone's name, so it will be no surprise that Hematite
is often used for blood purification. In fact, Hematite is a popular,
all-around purification stone. The stone itself is a form of iron oxide,
so it is possible early uses of Hematite in crystal healing involved
ingesting the stone. Of course, we don't recommend ingesting *any
stone*, even stones you might want to steep in water. Due to its iron
content, Hematite is also mildly magnetic. Most of the magnetic
Hematite you find on the market, though, has been doctored to
produce a more obvious magnetic quality. Hematite is a great stone to
use at the Earth chakra, which is a chakra just below the Root Chakra

---

18 This is mentioned in Diane Morgan's *Gemlore* (pg. 88). If garnet was said to light a vessel designed to carry people out
    of danger when humanity was being flooded nearly out of existence and then had to rebuild, then garnet is connected
    both to pomegranate seeds (birth and death) and floods as well (death and rebirth).

and is one of the energy circles recognized outside of the traditional, Western, seven-chakra system.

Use Hematite when you need to feel grounded. Wear Hematite as a bracelet or carry it in your pocket. Focus your thoughts on the course of your blood through your body as you thumb the Hematite you hold. Really feel your blood moving in your arteries and veins, and imagine it flowing clockwise from your heart, down through your right leg, into your right foot, and straight into the Earth like the root of a tree, then back up again through your left foot, up your left leg, and back to your heart. Focus on this until you can really feel the pulse of energy moving through your body with your blood and feel yourself ground to the Earth beneath you.

Herkimer Diamond: Herkimer Diamonds are not actually Diamonds, but rather a double-terminated rock or Quartz Crystal named for the area of New York where this clearest crystal vein was discovered and mined in the eighteenth century. Because these are Quartz, they carry all the same qualities as a Quartz Crystal and more: attunement with yourself and your intentions, focus on goals, clarity of vision, programming for manifestation, and sweeping out negative energy, as well as themes involving moving beyond the limitations of time and space. Because the stones are double-terminated Quartz stones with naturally occurring points on each end, they work as wonderful channels of energy if you are experiencing a blockage in any of your chakras. Just place the stone on the body so that one point of the stone is aimed upward and the other downward to get energy moving through the body again. These stones, like other high vibrational stones such as Moldavite, have a notorious history of "running away" when it isn't the right time for you to work with the stone's energy.

The double termination of Herkimer Diamonds makes them a great stone for attunement between two people. Just bring together the stones and program them as you normally would program a Quartz Crystal with your intentions for positivity. In fact, you might wish to write down statements between the two of you that align your goals and energy toward one another, and then hold the stone close to each other's hearts to attune to one another. Trade stones and keep them with you, or place them on a shelf where you will see them often to remind you of your mutual goals. The clarity of a Herkimer Diamond also makes them excellent stones for gazing, which is simply staring into a crystal and calming the mind or allowing the imagination to explore what it sees in the crystal's center.

Howlite: This trickster stone comes naturally in shades of white and blue such that it can resemble Turquoise to the unsuspecting stone connoisseur. It is a softer stone in general, so it is at risk of dissolving in water or mild acids like vinegar, and it is best to keep it out of liquids. Howlite is a great anxiety reducer. We like to wear Howlite beads around the wrist to transmute feelings of anger into vibrations of calm. As a white stone, it's also useful in the expanded chakra system *just above the Crown Chakra,* sometimes called the Halo or Soul Star Chakra. Hold a piece of Howlite above your head and imagine it radiating a pure white light down over you. It is protective and clarifying when worn in earrings as well.

Howlite is one of the most relaxing stones to use for sleep or meditation. Whenever Lune uses it with clients by placing it on their forehead near their hairline, they later remark, "What was that one you put on my forehead, because as soon as you did, I was out!" It helps us get into a lovely, trance-like state and is excellent to use with dream-work.

Jade: Of all the stones described in this chapter, Jade may be the oldest stone of significance in our written history. Sacred to the area around the Yangtze River Delta, Jade has been used by royalty in China since ancient times to ensure prosperity and calming influences, but Jade is by no means exclusively known to Chinese history. Celebrated for its beauty and the ease of sculpting it, Jade was used in sacred sites in Mexico and other parts of Latin America, New Zealand, and the British Isles. It decorated temples, was carved into spiritual sculptures, and was even manufactured into weaponry. Jade is generally considered lucky—particularly when it is given as a gift. Typically a pale green, Jade is a great Heart stone. For the purists out there, you will want to look out for Jade's (or Jadeite's) twin-cousin Nephrite, which is less expensive to mine and therefore sometimes crops up as a Jade substitute. Because Jade has been cherished by so many cultures for millennia, dating back as far as six thousand years ago, it is relatively easy to find antique Jade pieces set in jewelry that may bring with it years of prayer and associated support. Just remember to cleanse or smudge out any negative energies that may be attached to old pieces of Jade you may pick up from the flea market or antique store.

As Jade is known to be lucky to receive as a gift, this is a perfect stone to use to tap into the energies of generosity and blessings by gifting it to another. There is a certain magick in the dynamic of giving and receiving, and, while we should not give with the expectation of receiving, still the Universe does hold and honor balance.

Jasper: Jasper is one of the most versatile and diverse stones in any healing collection. It comes in just about every color of the rainbow and can therefore easily align with any of the chakras. Dendritic Jasper is often a light brown stone mottled with tree-shaped lines of black or darker brown. It can look like a forest landscape or an ocean at sunset. (Dendritic essentially means "spotted.") Though Jaspers come in all colors, perhaps the most popular are the red and orange varieties, which reinforce the grounding, physical roots of this Earthy stone. Jasper in general is great for the Root and Sacral Chakras and can support a sense of security and protection. It also makes a great tool for focusing mental and physical energy. We often use it to infuse an intention of overall body and cognitive wellness, such as just before beginning a new fitness or eating routine for overall health and well-being. It is also one of the easiest stones to come by due to its abundance.

Because Jasper has such a nurturing and supportive energy, it is a great stone to have with you all the time because you never know when you'll need it. It makes an excellent pocket stone or pendant for this reason, like a best friend who is always with you and has your back.

~~~~~~

Jet: While Jet is a very hard, stone-like substance, it is actually an organic material and not truly a rock. Jet is carbon-based, fossilized wood and generally is a softer substance than most stones. Ranging from a 2 to a 4 on Mohs' scale, Jet can be easily dissolved like a Pearl. Jet is sometimes called the "witch's stone" or "black amber,"[19] and of course the color jet black comes from this harder, charcoal-like substance. Because Jet is black and made of wood, it is good for connecting with the idea of Earth's abundance and longevity. It can be used on any chakra but is an ideal stone for the nondominant hand to dispel negative energy (while a piece of Clear Quartz crystal in the dominant hand can draw positive energy in at the same time). If you're inclined to follow the patterns of nature, Jet might be best used at the New Moon, when the night sky is dark.

We love this stone-like wood for Earth-based guided meditations or drum journeys. Set an intention to work with this stone as your guide and to honor all the souls and experiences which have come before you. You may also use it to overcome a fear of death or to honor the circle of life.

~~~~~~

---

19 According to Diane Morgan, author of *Gemlore: Ancient Secrets and Modern Myths of the Stone Age to the Rock Age,* "Jet is considered magically 'married' to amber and the two are often worn together, especially by modern day Wiccan priestesses." (Pg. 109).

Kyanite: This softer stone comes primarily in shades of blue or black but is found in green and orange as well. The black variety it is said to resemble a raven's wing. Black Kyanite is an excellent diffuser of negative energy, as it virtually sucks up all the emotional toxicity around it. Some say Black Kyanite is one of the few stones that does not need to be regularly smudged or cleansed as it is known to transmute negative energy. In its blue form, it is an excellent stone for the Throat or Third Eye Chakras, as they enhance our ability to communicate clearly, engage our spiritual selves, and visualize the present and future.

Kyanite crystals in all colors typically come in a spear or blade shape, so they make excellent wax pens to inscribe a wish into a pillar candle before you burn it, or dip a Kyanite point into molten wax to write an intention on a piece of slate. Its natural point and blade shape also make it easy to attach to a rod or the end of a pen to bring focus to any task, or you might suspend it from a string for dowsing. Wire-wrapping Kyanite spears into a crown or headband or threading them into a braid of sweetgrass or an herbal wreath are also great strategies for bringing Kyanite's energy into your home.

Labradorite: This beautiful, shimmering stone is perhaps best known for the glimmer it produces when it is waved under light, almost like the glittery, opalescent inside of an abalone shell. Primarily blue or blue-green, this stone seems to take on the colors of the aurora borealis under flickering light and can at times appear to be any color from mauve to blue to green to purple. We love this stone for heart-healing work, either as a palm stone or shaped into a heart, because its reflective, shiny appearance brings beauty and joy to whatever is near it. Many pieces of Labradorite are dark blue, and, therefore, they work wonderfully to clear the pathways of communication, allowing us to speak our heartfelt truths.

Imagine the iridescent flashes of color in Labradorite as mini electrical charges that can flash purpose, meaning, hope, or simply light in whatever direction you need it to shine. The flashes of light under the surface of the gray feldspar speak of the unseen. Set the intention to connect with that light beneath the surface.

Lapis Lazuli: Perhaps one of the oldest known stones for energy work due to its prolific use in Egyptian history (and beyond), this stone was once sacred to the royal and priestly classes. In fact, most of the earliest books (going back thousands of years) about the uses of stones and crystals are called lapidaries (from the Latin word meaning compendia for working with stones); Lapis Lazuli means literally "blue stone." True Lapis Lazuli is an azure stone with flecks of Pyrite visible within it. Sodalite, a similarly dark blue stone, is sometimes passed off as Lapis Lazuli, so look for that telltale Pyrite inclusion if you want real Lapis Lazuli. Its dark blue aspect makes it an excellent stone for the Third Eye and any work involving insight or intuition.

Imagine that the veins of Pyrite in this blue stone are channels of glowing gold showing you the way through a dark path. With this image in your mind, see yourself traveling a golden, shining path in a rich blue night until you find your way to a destination. Use this simple meditation for pathworking with Lapis Lazuli.

Larimar: This brilliant, sea-blue stone was rediscovered just a few decades ago on the shores of the Dominican Republic, where the ocean is the color of summer sky. It is often described as a rediscovery of the lost stones of Atlantis. The stone has bright blue and white whorls, a bit like the swells of the sea in a state of unrest. The idea that it is connected to the very same Atlantis mentioned by Plato himself suggests this stone is excellent for channeling and harnessing psychic energy and then directing that energy toward a clear intention. As a light blue stone, it is helpful for clear communication.

Wearing a Larimar necklace set in silver can help you focus and align the Throat Chakra.

Larimar has a very yin, feminine energy, and it really connects us to the softness of sea-foam paired with the unfathomable strength of the ocean. Use it to empower the feminine, receptive, intuitive, patient, compassionate, empathic, and nurturing qualities you possess. Find strength in softness and vulnerability, and embrace courage.

Lava Rock: Also known as Basalt, Lava Rocks are either Basalt pieces of solidified mulch excavated from volcanic sites. In its hardest form, a Lava Rock is Obsidian. The more porous Lava Rocks, such as Pumice and Scoria, are softer versions of this stone that serve many purposes. Because they come from volcanoes directly, they are inextricably connected to the element of fire and therefore concerned with passion and rapid transformation. Likewise, they are a deeply Earthy stone, since they come practically from the center of the Earth itself. Their rough shape gives them a sensory texture that can be physically grounding when you palm this stone or rub it softly over your skin. As a black stone, it's great for any of the chakras, but particularly the Root, as it firmly connects us to the ground beneath us.

Use this stone when you need to foster courage and strength in the face of adversity, or when you need to change or heal after a tragedy or loss.

Lodestone: These tricky stones must have seemed purely magical to those who first discovered them and put them to use! A Lodestone is a naturally occurring magnetized stone. Rich in iron, this stone is often used metaphysically to purify the blood or motivate the Root Chakra energies. This is an excellent stone when you feel like you are spiraling out of control and need to anchor yourself to feel secure.

As a magnet, it's also a ferociously attractive stone that you can use to amplify the drawing power of any intention you set.

You might find a shop selling Lodestone growing in spiky or almost fuzzy looking formations, or alternatively, as tumbled or raw stones. Regardless of the formation, these are incredibly powerful manifestation stones. Place one in the center of your grid, particularly a "fuzzy" one, and place stones around it (such as Pyrite or Jade, for abundance) to draw prosperity. Or use smaller pieces to create a box or square around a Lodestone sphere or tower to draw more energy to the center piece with your corresponding intention. Since Lodestones are magnetic, you might use one to pin an affirmation to your refrigerator to draw that energy to you every time you reach for a glass of milk.

Malachite: As one of the few specifically toxic stones in a healer's tool kit, Malachite calls you to be extremely careful when using it in your practice. Touching raw Malachite or keeping it close to your skin for any length of time can be poisonous, so use Malachite cautiously or as a visual aid and not a wearable object. Tumbled and polished pieces are less risky than the fibrous variety, but better to be safe. Never submerge this stone in water, not even for a room spray, as the toxicity of such a pretty stone can be easily forgotten and quite harmful.

This stone is a brilliant, verdant green, the color of forest leaves in the middle of summer or moss-covered stones near a waterfall. When tumbled, Malachite has rings or dapples like a tree stump or freckled skin, and its color makes it a particularly useful stone for connecting with nature.

This green stone is great for working with the Heart Chakra. Malachite helps you to change direction peacefully for your highest good. It has a lush energy, and it is excellent for manifesting things of beauty or luxury.

Meteorite: These literally celestial stones are sometimes stone, but are also often metal composites, usually nickel and iron, that originate in outer space and come to the Earth through the atmosphere as particles from comets and asteroids. Its mystical origin infuses this stone with a natural (or perhaps supernatural) symbolism, making it perfect for Third Eye and Crown Chakra work to align your goals and energies with a higher purpose. Connected to the stars above, Meteorite works wonderfully as a tool to draw Kundalini energy up the spine.

Place a piece of Meteorite on a shelf above your desk or bed, or in your line of sight where you might meditate or perform a physical routine like yoga or Tai Chi. You can also place it beneath your feet or hold it between the soles of your feet while sitting in the lotus position to draw higher purpose energy down into your root and align your aspirations for the future with the resources of your present. This is an excellent spiritual stone.

Moonstone: One of Araminta's first encounters with Rainbow Moonstone was discovering it in a New Age shop in a box labeled, "Past Life Stone." This icy blue or white stone is said to attract the attention of people with whom we have a soul connection. Even without that belief, though, it is easy to see why this shiny, opalescent stone attracts so much attention! Rainbow Moonstone is not technically Moonstone but is actually White Labradorite. In this book we call it Rainbow Moonstone because that is how you will find it labeled. True Moonstone is similar in that it is also feldspar, but typically has a more milky appearance without the blue, green, or orange flashes seen in White Labradorite. It may also have a silver sheen or luminous luster. True Moonstone comes in milky gray, peach, green, or even black varieties, and all carry a comforting, maternal energy. Its connection to the moon is in its very name, so Rainbow Moonstone is an easy tool for aligning with the cycles of nature, be they your physical or body cycles like biorhythms or the emotional cycles of life transitions. It is a stone which aids with intuition and is therefore a great stone for augmenting the Third Eye Chakra.

This is an excellent stone for work with healing the inner child. It can support you in going back to memories by virtue of the Third Eye and channeling maternal, supportive energy to your younger self.

Obsidian: This Lava Rock or Lava Glass is said to be one of the hardest stones you can excavate. It is excellent as a protection or shielding stone. This stone has been used in the manufacture of weapons and tools for millennia and appears as dishes or spearheads and knives in historical sites all over the world. It comes in many varieties, such as black, gold sheen, rainbow, mahogany, snowflake, and even colored pieces. Lune recently found a natural piece of Green Obsidian at a crystal event—previously she would never have believed natural Green Obsidian existed due to its rarity. Like Lava Rocks, this stone is both fiery and Earthy, bringing with it the symbolism of both rapid transformation and profound security and stability. This is a good stone for Root or Crown Chakra work as it has properties of both Fire and Earth.

Obsidian is great for scrying, or simply gazing. Get a disc of Obsidian about the size of your palm, invest in a carved Obsidian bowl that you fill with water, or choose a dark colored bowl and place tumbled Obsidian pieces at the bottom. Hold the bowl or disc near a flickering light like a candle, and simply gaze into it. What shadows or images dance across the surface? What do they mean to you? You do not need to see the future when you perform this activity. Let your mind dance with the light across the surface of the stone and see where your thoughts take you.

Onyx: The black variety of this stone is so black that it often appears silver due to the reflection of light on its surface. It can be confused with Hematite, but they are different stones entirely. Onyx reduces negativity and relieves anxiety. It is also a great dream tool. Perhaps because it resembles the night sky, this hard stone can be sewn into the hem of a pillowcase to aid with grounding and purposeful dreams.

Before going to sleep at night, gently touch the Onyx and say out loud, "I will remember my dreams." This sends a subconscious message that triggers your memory and increases the likelihood that you will remember your dreams. You can also ask the stone to help you answer a particularly vexing question while you sleep, such as "What should I do next with my life?" or "How should I handle this new relationship situation?" Then, when you remember your dream in the morning, write it down immediately. Give it some time and think about what your dream might be trying to tell you. If you kept your Onyx loose, carry it with you for the day and touch it from time to time to bring the dream memory back. As the day goes on, you may have new or emerging ideas about the symbols the dream is using to translate your intuitive self to your cognitive self. Listen carefully.

Opal: Opal comes in many colors, such as green, black, and pink, but Fire Opal takes the cake, visually speaking. With the sparkling sheen of Labradorite and the pale, iridescent shell coloring of an abalone shell, the sparkling fire caught within an Opal's glint can glitter red or orange against the paler opalescent background. Dark green opals often sparkle with the same flicker in the right light. What is particularly fascinating about Opal is the quantity of water it contains: Opal is a hydrated silica gel, meaning that this stone is sometimes home to up to 10 percent of its own mass in water; an Opal can actually "dry up" and lose some of that sparkle and sheen.[20] Though many prefer a Rose Quartz for the Heart Center, a brilliant, polished Green Opal with that opalescent sheen is Araminta's preferred stone for Heart Chakra alignment because of its watery composition. The water inside an Opal seems to resonate (just as the

---

20 Diane Morgan indicates in *Gemlore* that water actually leaks out of these stones over time, leading to that dried out look (131).

work done demonstrates how water molecules take on a shape based on the emotions you project into it[21]).

The beautiful flashes of light seen in Fire Opals can act like sparks of inspiration, ideas, creative thinking, or major shifts in perspective. Use this stone to conjure new ways of processing or looking at the world.

Pearl: This is an organic material that is created by a mollusk, such as an oyster, when an irritant or foreign body enters the creature and its secretions collect around it. As an organic substance, Pearls are actually a form of calcium carbonate, which is a very soft material— so soft that ancient Romans used to dissolve their pearls in vinegar or water to create a kind of health tonic.[22] One important aspect of Pearls in energy work is that the harvesting of a true, genuine Pearl requires that the mollusk that created it be killed. Since Pearls came into high fashion thanks to Queen Victoria, it is possible to find Pearls at antique stores and therefore collect Pearls that have long since been harvested rather than supporting the farming or harvesting industries of today. Pearls do come in different colors, including the very rare black Pearl. Very spherical Pearls are the most coveted as symbols of natural perfection. There are, however, freshwater and seed Pearls that are shaped more amorphously.

Pearls are great for connecting with our deepest selves and shadow selves. Holding or wearing pearls is a great way to slip into a deep meditation and connect with the voice of your soul.

---

21 It should be noted that water is in fact a crystal, and water responds visibly to the presence of intention. A study of water molecules' responses to the emotional states of those injecting the water with thoughts and intentions found that water changes its shape and color based on the emotion—happiness yielded brilliant, colorful, geometric crystal patterns. For more information about Masaru Emoto's experiments with water crystals, check out his books: *The Hidden Messages in Water* and *Water Crystal Healing*.

22 For further reading on this and other stones' history, we recommend Diane Morgan's book, *Gemlore: Ancient Secrets and Modern Myths from the Stone Age to the Rock Age*. Westport, CT: Greenwood, 2008.

Peridot: This cheerful stone is often yellow, yellow-green, or pale green and aligns with both the Solar Plexus and Heart Chakras for matters of creativity and love. The joy associated with this stone makes it useful for alleviating grief, despair, pessimism, hopelessness, sorrow, and guilt. In its yellowish forms, Peridot is reminiscent of sunlight or candle flames and can drive out the darkness that may be taking root in your heart and mind. This is also an intellectual stone, perhaps owing to its Solar Plexus connection, that can help you manifest creative solutions to challenges you face.

Use Peridot to create new intentions, reinforce old intentions, or embark on new learning experiences—particularly when you really want that learning to stick, such as when studying for a college examination or a licensure board test. This stone also releases resentment and jealousy, and it can remind you about your connections to others as it resonates with the relationship sector of your energy field.

Pyrite: Known more commonly as Fool's Gold, Pyrite bears a strong resemblance to gold in color and metallic luster. Unlike real Gold, though, Pyrite is brittle and flaky like gypsum. It typically forms in cubic clusters as rock crystals do. Real Gold is soft and pliable, whereas Pyrite is harder than Gold, with a Mohs rating of about 6 to 6.5. Chemically, Pyrite is actually an iron sulfide (not Gold at all), and that composition allows it to spark when struck, like flint. That's actually the source for its name, as "Pyrite" comes from the Greek word for fire: pyre. Pyrite is also the mineral that gives Lapis Lazuli its gold veins.

Pyrite helps you to relax into inspiration and abundance. Use Pyrite to manifest your personal wealth or how you perceive the wealth in your life. Wherever wealth in terms of material abundance is concerned, it is also helpful to imagine wealth as immaterial abundance, such as a wealth of creativity, energy, and health. Pyrite is a great stone for manifesting creation, like new art or writing projects, as well as for focusing your energy on positive health.

Quartz: Also called "rock crystal" or just plain old "crystal," Quartz is a clear or milky mineral that is abundantly available all over the world. It is also the material that makes up the classic "crystal ball" used by soothsayers and fortune tellers in both fictional and nonfictional worlds. Quartz Crystal is the quintessential crystal. It is used in everything from lasers to clocks to leverage its organizational composition and piezoelectric qualities for conductivity, vibration, and oscillation—all features of Quartz's super-organized, crystalline structure at the molecular level. Perhaps because it is one of the most abundant crystals, this is the single most popular and versatile gemstone you can obtain. It amplifies any intention or manifestation work you might be doing. Turn the crystal points toward the stones you wish to amplify in a grid, or turn the points outward to expand the energy to others. You may hold them in your hands with the points inward to draw energy to you to relieve burnout or points outward to expel energy from you to relieve stress. Rock crystal clusters will attract and hold energy for the moments you need it. Place a quartz crystal on a windowsill to gather the energy of the sun and moon, just be sure to keep it clean and dust free to maintain its luster and focus. Quartz Crystal is also a staple in nearly any energy work you might do, and it is the second of the palm crystals most healers use in drawing in or expelling energy during a standard relaxation session. (Jet or another black stone, such as Hematite or Black Tourmaline, is held in the other hand.)

Our biggest suggestion when working with this crystal is to remember to "program" or dedicate it to support your needs. It has become fashionable to wear Quartz Points as jewelry, but without infusing them with intention, they have the ability to work almost against your deepest goals. Simply tell the stone what you want it to do, or ask it to amplify only your Heart's desires.

Rose Quartz: Rose Quartz is a variation of standard Quartz Crystal, but it is made pink or rose-colored by the presence of various reddening minerals (like iron or other substances). Just be wary, as that Rose color can fade if certain varieties of this stone are left in the sunlight for prolonged periods. Unlike rock crystal which forms in spires and crystalline shards, Rose Quartz never (or perhaps only very rarely) naturally produces those pointy crystals. Rather, it is found in large hunks of semitransparent pink stone. Its rose color is reminiscent of the blush of new love on the cheek or in the heart where the blood rushes. Perhaps this is the connection energy healers make to align Rose Quartz with the Heart Center in addition to the green stones that would traditionally be used to support that chakra. Rose Quartz has been found in huge slabs, so it is not uncommon to discover a huge deposit of Rose Quartz that needs to be broken up in order to be used. One such magnificent twenty-pound Rose Quartz specimen came into Araminta's family in 1955 when her great-aunt, known to all as "Sweetie," found a volleyball-sized Rose Quartz chunk while rockhounding in the hills of Central Maine and gifted it to Araminta's grandmother. It sat in her grandmother's front yard for decades before it made its way to Araminta's own yard, where it currently resides. As you can see, Rose Quartz is easy to obtain and can host beautiful, loving ancestral memories.

Use Rose Quartz in your relaxation work for self-love and healing the heart. Rose Quartz is also a gift of love, so bestowing it on someone experiencing a hard time may contribute to supporting that person's wellness.

Ruby: While often imagined as the blood-red stone on the shoes of a famous character from the golden age of film, Rubies actually come in a variety of colors, including mauve, pink, purple, and even green. Its most commonly scarlet color links it to the Root Chakra and helps you to feel secure and abundant, but its vibrant red color does you one better: it also amplifies your sexuality and all matters of warming the blood. It is a high-energy stone which can amplify your energy, giving you a boost when you start to feel a little fatigued. Because this is one of the more precious stones, it is possible to find very valuable Ruby ring and bracelet settings to wear against your skin. It is advisable to wear Rubies close, as they have a strong influence on the aura. Set an intention into a wearable Ruby to amplify whatever you wish to manifest.

Tied to sexuality, Ruby also increases our attractiveness to others, as well as enhancing our overall sensory and social experiences. Choose Ruby when you wish to feel alluring in any way, whether or not you wish to attract and intrigue a new friend or lover.

Sapphire: Like Rubies, Sapphires are highly precious stones that can easily be found in expensive jewelry settings to be worn close to the auric field. These blue gems resonate with the Throat Chakra, opening lines of communication and clearing the air between two people. This stone can help alleviate feelings of being misunderstood. It's a conversation stone. Sapphires have been given throughout history as a popular engagement ring setting perhaps for that very reason, as their symbolic alignment works to keep dialogue open, clear, honest, and loving between two people or simply within yourself, harmonizing communication between mind and body or emotion and intellect. Sapphires are excellent for spiritual wisdom, and they were worn by the priestesses at the famous sacred site of the Oracle at Delphi. Don't expect every sapphire you see to be blue, though, as there are also green, black, pink, and yellow varieties of this mineral. In all its iterations, this crystal is great for intentions about prosperity, hope, wisdom, resilience, spiritual strength, and integrity. Wear it and speak your truth.

Use Sapphire to connect with your inner Higher Priestess or Hierophant when you want to "get serious" for a manifestation ritual.

Selenite: This form of gypsum, an exceptionally soft stone that easily dissolves in liquid and can splinter and chip if handled roughly, has become one of the most popular healing stones in the energy worker's tool kit for its incredible versatility and abundance. A pale, almost translucent white, Selenite is formed in an almost wand-like pattern such that it looks as if bands of straws have been laid on top of one another and compacted. Selenite is easily sculpted or shaped, and many Selenite fans use it in the form of a wand to point and direct its healing energy. Lune even calls a flat-sided Selenite wand a "squeegee for the etheric body." Selenite removes energy blocks in all the chakra centers and is extremely adept at attracting that energy (as well as dust). One major consideration when working with Selenite is its softness. On Mohs' scale, this stone is only a 2, which means it not only dissolves easily in liquid, it also can sometimes be shaped by your fingernails, leaving your stones vulnerable to dings and chips. It's an excellent stone for the Crown Chakra, with its ability to connect you to the moon for which it is named. It represents purification and release of inhibitions.

Try holding a Selenite wand near light and point one of the tips toward the chakra zone you wish to heal or energize. Imagine that you are pulling the light through the Selenite wand and into your body where, like a windmill turbine, it spins your chakra to its purest state. Another option is to lie on your stomach and place a long, solid rod of Selenite on your spine. Let it amplify the path of energy from Root to Crown as it amplifies your Shakti.

Smoky Quartz: Another adaptation of rock crystal, Smoky Quartz is formed much like Clear Quartz, only with either pale brown or dark black coloring. The darkest specimens of Smoky Quartz actually contain irradiated aluminum deposits. Like Clear Quartz, Smoky Quartz is widely available and has a versatile function. Many people choose to work using Smoky Quartz specifically with elements of the underworld or afterlife or when working with our

Jungian Shadow selves, those parts of ourselves that represent the opposite manifestation of how we present to most people we meet in the world. The dark quartz allows the practitioner to connect with the amplifying qualities of Clear Quartz Crystal with the added benefit of darkness, bringing it into the realms of night. It is a highly protective stone because it infuses your sense of self-actualization, reminding you that you can be safe and successful while connecting with others.

Though protective, Smoky Quartz never feels harsh and instead has an almost warm and cozy feeling, like being safely in your home during a storm. Place it in your home near the front door to keep out negative vibes. As you walk into your home, pause and look at the stone with intention. Say to yourself: I allow my energy to be cleansed by this stone and easily shift into comfort mode.

Sodalite: This blue, white-speckled stone is often misidentified as Lapis Lazuli as both are a dark, navy blue shade with veins of different colors. Blue Sodalite is great for communication and the Throat Chakra. It also opens your intuitive center and can symbolically open pathways of communication between your emotional and intellectual minds, the higher and lower minds, or the innate and conscious minds. Sodalite is often used in creativity work, as it is aligned with the conduit for inspiration, drawing in positive energy with each breath.

Hold Sodalite in your hand or place it over the Throat on top of the skin to breathe in positive energy (literally, to inspire), and breath out your truth and purpose. Use it to harmonize your inner, social, and emotional knowing with your more logical, fact-based awareness.

Tiger's Eye: This shiny, banded, brown, yellow, gold, and maroon stone is called Tiger's Eye because its tawny shimmer is reminiscent of a cat's eyes. Its connection with eyes supports its connection to visualization practices, and it helps its wearer or worker to promote clarity of vision and unblock emotional static by *seeing* through it. This stone works well for any of the lower, physical Chakras: Root, Sacral, and Solar Plexus. It can also help the Third Eye. Its strong roots in security and creative manifestation allow it to easily remove self-doubt and strengthen your sense of self-worth. Use this stone to boost your self-esteem when you're feeling low or to set intentions around security and safety.

Use Tiger's Eye to work with the Third Eye and Solar Plexus to imagine yourself as the version of you that you are manifesting in accordance with your Will and to authentically resonate with your personal truth.

Topaz: This silicate crystal comes in many shades of clear, blue, or yellow, and therefore connects with the Crown, Throat, and Solar Plexus Chakras. Wearing this stone on your person or in your pocket boosts your drive to succeed and helps you gain recognition for the value you contribute to your community. These stones are confidence boosters and help you to improve your sense of self-assurance. In all its colors, Topaz is also the stone of forgiveness. If you are troubled by rage, frustration, or resentment, use this stone to set an intention to forgive with grace.

Because the internal structure of Topaz is two-directional, it can establish energy flow in the subtle system, clearing what doesn't support your highest good and channeling energy flow toward you that does.

Turquoise: This stone was sacred to the Egyptians and Native Americans as far back as 6000 BCE. It has been found at sacred and historical sites in amulets and other utensils that adorned tombs. This stone is thought to be a super-healer, and, when worn around the neck, it is particularly healing to matters of the Throat and all things related to clear and coherent communication. It is a lucky stone when given as a gift, so carry your gifted Turquoise to draw in healing and positive emotional energy. This stone also energizes all the chakras in much the same way Clear Quartz Crystals amplify the work of any stones it is nearby.

Working with Turquoise during times of transformation is ideal. Whether life has forced some kind of change on you or you are making your own deliberate changes, Turquoise is a stone which effectively helps you move through that time.

ACKNOWLEDGMENTS

Araminta Star Matthews would like to thank so many people for the manifestation of this book, beginning first and foremost with her dear friend Jillian, without whom this book would truly not have been possible. Thank you, Jillian, for not only thinking of me but for sticking with me through the shadows. I also need to thank those who supported me along the way, including Shellie Cook, Kimberly Moore, Emily Cerda, Shiva Darbandi, Joel Norris, Caitlin Southwick, Will Sharpe, Abner Goodwin, Bonnie Gould, Heidi Jackson, Vickie Gould, Hugo Villabona, and everyone at Art of Awareness and The Bridge Studio. I want to give a special shout-out to the following people: my friend and colleague Anne Fensie, for digging me out of an editing slump when I really needed the help; my dearest fellow BFA ("Bachelor of F***ing Around") Jacob Scott Ware, for relentless edits to my redundant words; and my soul-sister, Heather Nunez-Olmstead, whose unstoppable optimism was a beacon for every contribution I made to this work. Most of all, I need to thank and honor my daughter, Zelie, who is the brightest Star in my darkest sky. Finally, a special thank you to each of you who has picked up a copy of this book: You all have the power within you to manifest wellness. Take a breath. Turn your attention inward. Slow down. It's all right there in your center. Thank you for reading.

Lune Innate (Jillian) would like to honor the following people: first, my Nanny Carole and Auntie Dina for the major role they directly played in introducing me to intentions and energy. Carole first taught me to be sure to put my new Moonstone ring on my windowsill so it could be cleansed and changed by the moonlight. Dina, you are my first best friend, and I'm forever grateful for all the times you stayed up all night with me dancing on the beach under a full moon and charging candles! I'd also like to honor my mother, Gaye, for being my greatest teacher; while not incredibly spiritual, you taught me to write messages to our passed-on loved ones and burn them to carry the messages to the etheric realms. I want to honor my father, Robert, for being so human and never limiting me and my brother, Corey, for the way we share so much of each other's paths. I feel so much gratitude and love to Grigory for his incredible support, as well as to our son Howel for just being awesome. Huge thanks and love to Araminta for being side by side with me on this journey, and for her brilliance, realness, and loving encouragement. You're the best! Thank you, Joanne, for being an amazing teacher and encouraging me to follow my higher guidance! Finally, I have to thank every single soul who has supported this journey. I'm sure many who read this will be those who may have first "met" me on YouTube, and I couldn't be more honored by the opportunity to be of some support and to build such beautiful connections. For my lovely, incredible clients and for the friendships that have blossomed, I'm so very grateful from the bottom of my heart.

ABOUT THE AUTHORS

Lune Innate is an Esoteric Healing Arts Teacher, Master Level Practitioner, and Spiritual Content Creator with presently over 100K subscribers to her YouTube channel: The Lune INNATE. Her introduction to subtle energy was via her grandmother and aunt, and along her path she has received Master Teacher Level Reiki, Crystal Healing Practitioner, and Sacred Earth Energy training, in addition to her personal studies on Astrology, Symbolism, The Subconscious Mind, Hermeticism, and Spiritual Alchemy.

Born in New Jersey and living ten years in New York City, Lune is now based in South Florida where she teaches Healing Arts and guides clients on their spiritual path, both locally and internationally, as well as hosting events and retreats in various locations of the United States and beyond.

Lune's passions lie in empowering individuals who are on a path of personal and spiritual development by using practical and applicable methods to bring harmony to their lives while aligning with their Soul's desires of experience. It is her greatest honor to be of even the smallest support to someone along their personal life path.

Araminta Star Matthews has a Master of Fine Arts in Creative Writing from National University and a Bachelor of Fine Arts in the same discipline from the University of Maine at Farmington. She also holds certificates in digital curation, career development facilitation, and teaching. In addition to writing, she works as an instructional designer at a university developing and supporting the creation of instructional content for higher education courses. She also teaches Creative Writing for the University of Maine at Presque Isle, online.

She began her writing career in the horror genre, writing young adult, supernatural fiction. While this genre still holds a place in her heart, she is moving toward more practical content, such as holistic wellness and personal development guides. She has coauthored with Stan Swanson and Dr. Rachel Lee to produce the alternative writing instructional guide, *Write of the Living Dead,* and she has recently worked with The Lune Innate to produce a crystal self-care and wellness book.

Because Araminta can't bring herself to sit still even for a moment, she spends her spare time (when she is not teaching or writing or editing) playing MMORPGs, reading (mostly Romantic through Modernist period classics), and inventing. She is also a lifelong learner and routinely takes courses in disciplines that interest her, including yoga teaching, crystal certification, Reiki, web development, animation, and digital curation.

Mango Publishing, established in 2014, publishes an eclectic list of books by diverse authors—both new and established voices—on topics ranging from business, personal growth, women's empowerment, LGBTQ studies, health, and spirituality to history, popular culture, time management, decluttering, lifestyle, mental wellness, aging, and sustainable living. We were recently named 2019's #1 fastest growing independent publisher by *Publishers Weekly*. Our success is driven by our main goal, which is to publish high quality books that will entertain readers as well as make a positive difference in their lives.

Our readers are our most important resource; we value your input, suggestions, and ideas. We'd love to hear from you—after all, we are publishing books for *you*!

Please stay in touch with us and follow us at:

Facebook: Mango Publishing
Twitter: @MangoPublishing
Instagram: @MangoPublishing
LinkedIn: Mango Publishing
Pinterest: Mango Publishing

Sign up for our newsletter at www.mango.bz and receive a free book!

Join us on Mango's journey to reinvent publishing, one book at a time.